William Czappa

The Rules of Running a Successful Business

First Edition
October 24, 2018

Published in the United States by

ARC Publishing.
2800 N. Frederic
Burbank, Ca. 91504
(818) 846-5820 email **czappasstudio@gmail.com**
Web: www.czappasart.com
or Google: czappa

**Copyright 2018
William Czappa
All Rights Reserved**

No part of this book can be reproduced without the permission of the copyright owner. The short stories included and others not included, are available for purchase for your promotions.

Photo credit and all artwork;
William Czappa

ISBN-13:
978-1729619087

ISBN-10:
1729619088

Copyright pending
Names have been changed to protect the innocent if any are similar it is purely by accident. Spelling errors may be intentional or just errors.

Book code9242019414

Dedication

I would like to dedicate this book to all the wonderful customers that stayed with us through the years, recommended us and made it all possible. Also to all the employees that worked here over the years, some 125 of them. Also, I have to thank LRH and Wise International, who's business technology made us last longer and be more successful than most of our competitors.

ARC TV 2012

About the Author

Czappa owned ARC TV electronics business in Burbank California for 35 years. William began his career repairing color TV sets in 1969 for RCA service company. After working there for several years he opened his first independent repair store, Frodies Place, in Culver City Ca, where he grew up. In 1983 he took over H&G TV, renamed it ARC TV and ran it till he sold it January 15th, 2018.

He opened that business so that he could finance his other interests. William is also a California Visual artist and used the store to finance his art work so he wouldn't have to be a slave to the gallery system. He has been making sculptures from found objects since the sixties.

He began writing short stories in 1989 and began sending them to his growing art collector mailing list and then to his TV customers.

In 1987, The Burbank Leader first published one of Czappa's stories and for a short time he wrote a column for them featuring his stories. Since then, over 25 of his stories and other publications have been published in the Burbank Leader, the Burbank Times, the Tolucan and the Latest Magazine and other sites on line.

His 50 year retrospective of his art work was held at the Creative Art Center in Burbank and February, 2016.

There are three documentary shorts on Vimeo and YouTube about William, his work and the shop. (*Videos of the retrospective and the documentary shorts are on the net. Just Google Czappa Vimeo or Czappa YouTube*).

ARC also became ARC Gallery showing over 65 pieces of Williams work exclusively. The TV shop and gallery has been in several TV shows, like Storage Wars, and the Hulu show, Casual.

After selling the shop he is now concentrating on his art and writing. The shop continues under new management but without the art work.

ARC Gallery 2012

Other books by this author are available on Amazon.com

The Trials, Tribulations of Running a Small Business.
Why I sold my business after 35 years. Stories about my employees, challenges of running a business and business tips.

Tech Techniques
A book about his 50 years in the repair industry. Rules that you learn the hard way about repairing things.

Holidaze
A book of his humorous short stories about vacations and Holidaze while growing up in Culver City Ca.

Assembled in America
A book about is career as an artist with autobiography and 50 photos of his work with explanations.

The eBay Users Handbook
After doing eBay for over 18 years, I thought I would share all the tips and techniques I had learned. And offer a step by step user guide to make the first time eBay seller a pro right from the start.

About this book

After running my last business for 35 years, I realized that there are rules for running a business successfully.

First let me point out that being successful does not always mean making a lot of money. Success can be many things, like helping lots of people or making a lot of art work that people enjoy seeing. It can be keeping hundreds of people employed for many years. It's not always about making a lot of money.

There are huge corporations and individuals that have tons of money. But are they really successful? Are they admired or are they thought of as a con artist or something less?

If you know these rules, you will be successful to the extent that you apply them and you will fail to the degree you ignore them. So if you are about to start a business or just interested in improving the one you're already in, or you are taking over as a manager of a division of a business, these rules can make things run much smoother and lead to greater profits and success, whatever you conceive that to be.

Although it's written mostly for a smaller business, you'll see some of the mistakes larger corporations often make, because they don't know all of these rules either.

I wrote an earlier book about the rules of repairing things as I discovered that good technicians followed certain rules that were the basis of their success.

And in a similar manor, there are rules for running a successful business too, no matter what size.

I learned them by trial and error and just simply observing other businesses and noticing the things they were doing, either right or wrong, that were affecting their success or lack of. And by taking courses at Wise International.

Many of the examples will be things I learned running a TV and home electronic service business, my personal art gallery (housed in that business) and being a contemporary artist all my life. I also had an earlier successful repair business for four years and several home based businesses which were total failures. And now, having discovered, and have written down these rules, I know why. So a lot of examples of these rules will be referenced to those businesses.

I have also included a whole section on some unusual advertising ideas you can use that I discovered, or may give you new ideas of your own.

So without further a due, let's get into it.

Table of contents

1. Find the Right Business for You & Your Desires — 1
2. Always Be in Good Communication — 5
3. Don't Cause a Break in Communication — 10
4. Manage Your Business by using Statistics. — 15
5. Find and Keep Sending out Great Advertising — 20
6. Always Give Customers More Than They Paid for — 43
7. Find and Keep Great Employees — 45
8. Weed out Antagonistic Employees — 49
9. Have Great Training in Place & Lots of it — 51
10. Write Good Policies and Make them Known — 54
11. Be Able to Take Advice and listen to people — 55
12. Have Your Accounting in Order — 57
13. Run an Ethical Business — 60
14. A Real Example of what <u>Not</u> to Do — 62
15. Check List if you're Taking Over an Existing Business — 68

Appendix

I. Why Fix Things? — 70
II. The Pink Card — 73
III. More Junk Mail flyer — 74
IV. 30 Day Thank you Letter — 77
V. An anytime one page story, "Baseball" — 80
VI. A Holiday Story, "RCA Hollywood Christmas" — 82
VII. An Anytime Story, "Finding Ginger" — 95
VIII. A Summer Story, "The Barbeque" — 100
IX. A Holiday story, "A Catalina Christmas" — 105

Chapter 1

Find the Right Business for You and Your Desires

There's nothing more painful than being in the wrong business. Whether you're a business owner or an employee, having to go do something every day that you hate is a recipe for an unhappy life. So this information also applies to working people as well.

I recall a story of a dentist who, after spending thousands of dollars and investing years and years to become a dentist, gave it all up because he hated doing that work every day. Why did he go through all that in the first place? His mom wanted a dentist in the family. He ended up working for a non-profit helping people, for much less money, but he was now enjoying his life.

So that's the most important issue, because when you really enjoy doing something it comes through to your customers. You can just see it and feel it.

How do you find what you want to do? Well take a look at your life. What class did you enjoy the most while in school? What hobbies were the most interesting to you? What kind of magazines have you had subscriptions to?

What subjects are you most interested in?

You could also make a list of things you like to do and things you hate to do. Like, do you like to work with numbers? Then accounting might be a good fit. Can you stand being around sick people? Then the healthcare industry might work.
Do you like to cook? Check out the food industry. I like to cook, but I don't want to do it all day long.

Once you find out what you would like to do, then go visit people in that profession. Find out what it's really all about, what the potentials are, what would it take for you to be in that field? What's the pay like? Then, if possible, work for someone in that field for awhile if they accept assistants, someone to clean up perhaps. See if you really like it.

What do you want to have?

Then, the most important thing, make a detailed list of what you want to "have" in your life. Be very specific, like how big of a home do you want, where do you want to live? How much money do you want to have in the bank? Do you want to own a yacht? Do you want to hang out with important people? What part of town do you want to live in?

Now this is very important. Because the business our profession you choose will determine if that business will be able to provide you those things.

I have a friend who came to California to become a famous well paid artist. He wanted to make lots of money and hang out with wealthy art collectors and celebrities.

He already knew what he wanted to <u>do</u> every day that would make him happy, make art, but what he didn't figure out was, what kind of art he would have to make to have those other things in his life.

Instead he made art that only he liked, art that was political and often cynical. And not many people where interested in owning that kind of art. He became more and more unhappy and after many years of struggle, living in a factory building having to wash up in a bathroom sink, he ended up attacking the gallery system because they were not giving him what he wanted. He finely ended up moving to Florida and gave up on the whole idea of making a living that way.

I also wanted to have an important gallery sell my work for me too. But I also didn't want to have to conform to what the "gallery system" usually demands, and that is 20 versions of one style of art. There are artists who have been making the same version of a style of art for 25 years or more. That just wouldn't have made me happy.

So you have to align those things you need and want in life with the business or profession that you want to be in. They have to line up if you intend to be happy.

What kind of business structure do you want to be in?

Another important question also comes up. Should you run your business as an individual, as a partnership or as a corporation. The simplest thing to do is run it as an individual, because you get to make all the decisions but have all the responsibility yourself.

Having a partner helps share the load, but it's the most difficult thing to do. In fact most friends that go into partnership running a business end up not being friends. I had several partners, in my first business and although we're still friends, we did have some difficult times and I ended up buying them out. The last partner I had, bought me out, because I ended up marrying one of his girl friend's and because of that, he couldn't work with me anymore.

But if you do go into a partnership, at least write down everything in painful detail. Who's responsible for what, if one partner has invested more, does he get a higher percentage back? What hours is everyone required to work? Who handles the finances? Get this down in detail signed sealed and delivered. And then, have a meeting every so often and go over the agreement, make sure everyone is still happy with it and make adjustments as necessary.

I opened a Herbalife business with my daughter and her husband and soon realized they were using up all of the stock that I paid for.

Forming a corporation is safe and there is some tax advantages, it's harder to be personally sued and corporations get audited by the IRS less often. It's also cool to put .Inc on the end of your business name. But you have at least two other people on the board of directors. That can be silent family members, or people who are more active participants. But what every you do once again, get everything down in writing.

So the first rule is, find the right business for you and make sure it will provide you with what you need in life.

Chapter 2

Always Be in Good Communication

Now once you have found your business, the first and most important rule for running it is, to be in communication with your customers and your employees.

This is not a book on how to learn how to communicate, there are courses for that, the best one being at a company called, Wise International. Their courses break down every part of the communication cycle and you drill each one of them. I have done them and highly recommend those courses and sending your employees there too, especially ones who deal directly with the public, they are extremely valuable. And the courses are a lot of fun to do. There are huge corporations that offer those same courses right on their premises.

Now let me explain a little about what I mean by communication. What goes on for communication in our society today is a joke. Try talking to someone who has their attention fixed on their cell phone for instance. Many people are upset with these news shows, like Fox. CNN and MSNBC because when they have a panel of opposing views, no one is listening to each other. Their just yelling. That's not communication, it's yelling, no one's listening.

Well there are also rules for communicating too. Being in communication means that you have the attention of the person you are talking to. It means that you say things clearly and see if they understand and acknowledged what you said. It also means that you listen and understand what they said to you. It means you talk to people in a way that makes them feel they're important. And it means letting people finish their thought without interrupting them. It means not talking down to people. You could also say, "being a good listener." This does take some practice, for some people a lot of practice.

At this point it would be good to just go out and have a look at people talking to each other. Go to a restaurant of some public place with lots of people. Are at least think about who you enjoy talking to and who you try to avoid, like the lonely neighbor that never lets you get a word in edgewise, and won't let you leave while he has to tell you, in painful detail, something that happened to him the other day.

You could also have lunch with someone and film the person you're with while you have a conversation. Then after words run it back and really notice their expressions when you're talking. Then have them film you while you talk and then play it back. Or just go up to friends and ask them to tell you how is it to have a conversation with you?

Have a look at how you talk to people, do you give them your full attention? Do you let them finish their sentences without interrupting them? Do you talk clearly and see if they seem to be understanding what you're saying? Do you let them know that you got what they said, in other words acknowledge them?

Now communication includes mail and emails too. Do you have friends that never acknowledge that they got your email? I make sure I answer any and everyone that emails me or writes me a letter, even if it's just to say, "Got it." Even on Facebook, if someone likes something I posted, or makes a comment on something I posted, I at least click on the **like** button so they know I saw their comment.

You need to be a little more careful when sending emails, because people cannot see your face or tone of voice. So if you put something in caps, (To call attention to a word), they may think you're yelling at them. And humor can also be lost or misconstrued. Sometimes emojis can help.

Make sure that you're not using technical words that people may not understand. If you must, give the definition in the letter or the ad. And you don't want to write things that may upset some people. If you're not in a political business you would never disparage one political party or another religion. A good thing to do with advertising is to have several people read it over to make sure you're message is clear before releasing it.

As I said, this is not easy for some people to learn, but it is extremely important. Although doing a course is a simple and thorough way of boosting your communication skills, just working on it every day can help.

Here is an actual example someone using them in a tense situation. George (my counter person), was also someone well trained in communication skills. One day he really shined when two rough looking guys showed up looking for trouble.

Their mother was an accountant for one of our customers and she noticed two identical charges in her client's bank account. She thought we ripped him off. So these goons were going to straighten it all out. They seemed to be high on something and George just calmly sat down with them, pulled the receipts out and got them to see that our customer had two identical machines that had the same problem, so naturally the price was the same. He pointed out the serial numbers were different, the dates were different etc. He <u>patiently</u> got through to them with very calm <u>unemotional</u> communication and by the time they left we were all shaking hands and happy as a bug in a rug.

A lot of businesses know that this is important and so they force their employees to say hello to everyone that walks in the door. And you as a customer usually get this unnecessary hello that you are now obligated to answer. It would be better not to do this at all if it's not sincere because you're just wasting people's time. It actually works against you.

There are also some interesting quirks some people have. Some have some strange habits you'll have to deal with. For instance, there's the person who asks you a question, but before you finish answering it, they ask another question. Then before you finish answering that, they ask another.

Another type is the person who doesn't like to originate communication. I was dating a very attractive woman once who dumped me because I was not talkative enough. She wanted to be with someone who did all the work. Another friend, who had a similar problem, would carefully listen and not originate any communication. Whenever I talked to him on the phone, I would have to occasionally say, "Are you still there?"

Years later I found out he had been running a very successful furniture business for years and he never mentioned it.

One other interesting person was a barber who had his shop next to mine. If I asked him a question it would take him 24 hours to answer me. He had so much communication that had to come out first, that he had to get that all out before he could take anything in. So he would show up the very next day and answer me. A very interesting case.

I got my water from a water store for years for my home and the business. But the guy running it was very unpleasant and had an attitude that seemed to indicate that I was bothering him. He often wouldn't say hello or even thank you. So I finally got fed up and found another supplier that was pleasant.

I wanted to leave a negative feedback for him on Yelp, not to hurt his business but to help him and make it a more pleasant experience for his other customers. But I couldn't even find the store on Yelp.

So to have a successful business make sure that you and any employee, who talk to the public or trains other employees, has great communication skills. This alone will make you lots of money and keep people coming back in.

Chapter 3

Don't Cause a Break in Communication

If the best thing to do is **be** in communication with people, the worst thing you can do is **break** that communication. How do you cause a break in communication? You go out of communication by not communicating, or doing something that is out of your customer's reality.

For instance, you promise you'll deliver the product at a certain time or at a certain price. Then you can't deliver it on time or meet that price and you don't bother to call to tell them. They find out when they come in to pick it up. You can cause a break by having a rude person call a customer. Or you finish the repair and hand their unit back with a scratch on it, or part of it is not working, the job is incomplete. You do a good job on the repair, then run over their sprinkler head or get dirt on their carpet. You make an appointment for a service call, then forget to do it and they have to call you to remind you. One customer was upset because I didn't wipe my feet on the door mat before I walked in his home.

From then on I always wiped my feet on everyone's door mat. And if I saw they had all their shoes lined up by the door, I would ask if they wanted me to take my shoes off.

Another customer was upset because I smoked a cigar on the way over to her house. When I came back with her TV a few days later, she said the smell made her sick and she got the flue. Bad breath and body odor can cause one too.

Here is an actual example I heard about recently, two techs went out to deliver and install a brand new microwave oven. They borrowed the customer's expensive dining room chairs, without asking. They installed the microwave putting unnecessary holes in their expensive cabinets. Then an hour later, she tries to use the new microwave and it doesn't work.

The customer comes back to the shop to get their old microwave back, because now they don't trust that the repair was correctly estimated, only to find it's sitting there all torn apart and parts taken out.

This led to a bad review on Yelp and in fact, every bad review is a **break in communication**. So if you want to know how one is created, go read some bad reviews, that will tell you a lot about what not to do and what people do expect.

The good reviews tell you what people appreciate. Now sometimes the customer creates the break because there reality does not align with your business. A customer came in late in the afternoon to have his TV repaired. We had a check out charge, due to the costs of really accurately estimating a repair, we have to invest our time and money.

He didn't like the <u>amount</u> of that charge, walked out mad and left a bad review. Even though I was polite and tried to explain why we had to charge an estimate charge. So sometimes you can't do anything about it, even if you're polite and explain everything to people. And when you get a bad review you should always answer it, even if it's a positive review, thank them for the positive reviews to.

A poorly designed web site can cause a break in communication if it's hard to navigate. Poorly designed web sites waste people's time and just make them upset, as well as automatic phone systems. To use my medical insurance it takes a minimum of 5 minutes to get to the person I need to talk to. It often hangs up on me before I get to that person. They make me jump through a whole bunch of hoops to get to the person I need to talk to. Now if I call my Pizza guy though, he instantly has my address. How does a major insurance company not have that technology?

One service shop I know of, gives everyone an unreasonable estimate of how long it will take to do the repair, then they don't bother to call them when they can't meet that deadline. When the customer calls him again, he always says, "It'll be ready tomorrow" and then doesn't make sure it's ready tomorrow. Then the next day makes them call him back again instead of calling them and following through. This is a guaranteed way to get a bad review and an angry customer. If you charge a check out charge, this can also lead to a charge back as well. Not to mention a lost customer.

I got a customer once because a competitor refused to answer his question. He simply wanted a <u>rough</u> idea of what it might cost to repair his TV.

The other shop said, "Just bring it in." The customer repeated, "I just want an idea of what it could cost?" the other shop said again, "Just bring it in." This went on a few more times. The customer brought it to me instead.

Another customer complained that he called a service shop who's technician was so rude to him that he asked to speak to a manager. The manager gets on the phone and he's talking to him even ruder then the employee.

So you can prevent breaks in communication by having clear polices about pricing and how long it takes to deliver a product. I had a policy that said, "If it isn't written it isn't true." I also avoided out right promises and if asked how long something might take I would say, "It usually takes…,It should be done by…, In other words I never say, "It will definitely will be ready by…,or "It's always done by….
Because I have to rely on other companies delivering a part to me on time. There're things that are out of my control. If I do ever say "for sure," it will be done at a certain time, I will make sure that it's done by that time. I'd walk it through myself.

And remember too much mail or email can work against you. I cut a coupon for Michaels for a discount on art supplies and before I new it my email was flooded with ads every day, sometimes twice a day. And putting people on long hold times and then keep repeating your advertising is not going to gain you any friends.

And occasionally you will see an advertisement that is so artsy, that you can't figure out what they're actually selling. The message is what's important in an ad. To make people try to figure out what you're trying to sell them is not going to help your business.

So good polices, well trained staff, and not over promising things, keeping customers informed and up to date, will prevent most breaks in communication.

Please Stand By   *1994*

Chapter 4

Manage your Business by Using Statistics

Successful businesses manage their business based on statistics. Every department and every employee should have a statistic. How can you measure how well a department is doing or a person is producing if you don't measure their output? To not manage this way means that the guy doing the most producing may leave in disgust while the lowest producer keeps getting advanced, because he is good at telling jokes or Sally is really cute.

So besides being the fair way of managing, it's the way that will lead to greater success. Now this is not a book about how to use these kinds of tools either, that is a whole different book. And places like Wise International already have courses on how to manage by stats and I highly recommend learning that data fully.

But I can at least give you an idea how managing by stats works. And by the way, I have found that people who don't like to keep stats, are people that are usually not very good producers.

Because they know instantly that the stat is going to show you that they're not doing very much.

First, each employee keeps track of his own stats. And each week, he posts how much output he produced on a graph. Even a janitor can have a stat, his might be how many square feet of floor got cleaned or how many offices got cleaned.

You then get some graph paper and post the date on the bottom line and on the vertical line you have the amount produced. The top is the amount the most that post could usually post in a week, (If it's a weekly graph). So say the post could make 40 items in a week, you put 45 or 50 on the top line, then dived it all the way to zero at the bottom. Then each week he would post how many got made. As the weeks go on, you then draw a line from each point on the graph to the next point. If it's dropping you put it in red and if it's going up you put it in black.

So for an individual, by keeping track of how many phone calls he made, or how many parts he manufactured, he can now try to get more efficient on doing his job and try to increase that amount. And that is very satisfying to a person who produces, because he can see it. He can also see that if the stat is going down he can have a look at what changed and fix it. Rewards can also be offered for high stats. You can make a game out of it.

And this is important, as a manager you can also compare how this employee is doing compared to other employees who are or were on that same post.

Now let's take an example for the owner or manager. You have a state on gross income. Add up everything that was sold month and that is what the company produced for that period. Now say the stat is going down, what do you do? You go look over the other stats and see which one has gone down.

You notice that the amount of money spent on advertising has dropped or the number of promo pieces sent out has dropped. Well, if you had ads that where working and you suddenly stopped them or cut down on them, or changed them, what would you expect to happen? In a larger company you may find that the person putting out the ads, stopped doing what was working and tried something new. So you get that advertising that was working back in and the gross income state should then go back up.

It could also be that the change in advertising made the income go up, well keep doing that then.

Cash Bills Graph

Now if don't want to do any of this at least have a cash bills graph. Probably the most important graph. Every month you add up how much money came in, (your gross income for that month) and post it on the graph. Then you add up all the money you spent for that month and post that on the graph (I liked to post cost in green). Now the difference is roughly your profit. Those lines should never cross.

Now you have to interpret them too. For instance you may, for instance, one month pay for an increase in stock or buy a chunk of advertising. But, if it's a wise investment, the income graph should increase over time to pay for it. So if these two lines stay apart and don't cross, you are going to be making a profit.

Now there is more you can do with this data and I believe Wise International is the only place that offers it. They offer pamphlets, books and whole courses on this subject. So I can only give you a rough idea how this works here.

It turns out that every part of your business is in a "Condition." If things are going along fine gradually increasing, that would be a Normal Condition. If suddenly income drops, that would be a "Danger" or "Emergency Condition. If they suddenly go steeply up, that would be an "Affluence Condition."

Now the slant of the line on your graph tells you what condition you're in. And there's a formula for each one of these conditions and all you have to do is look up the formula in the book, follow the steps of the formula, and the stat should go back up and lead you right into the next highest condition. You then follow that condition formula and it should keep going up.

And this is one of the most important things I learned about these conditions, When your gross income goes down the first thing many people, or business's do, is cut back on advertising. You can and should hold down costs on other things, but not on advertising.

That is a violation of the Emergency Formula. If your gross income is going down you had better advertise. If there is one big reason businesses fail, it is this, income drops so they stop or cut back on advertising.

From 1983 when I first opened my business, it was a rocked ride. We didn't need to spend very much on advertising during that period. But then the trade agreements like NAFTA kicked in and we suddenly had cheep TVs, VCRs and Stereos coming in from China. We handled it by increasing our advertising and improving it too. Mean while our competitors were dropping like flies. In the eighties there where at least 6 pages of TV repair shops in the phone book, by the teens, it dropped to ¼ page of ads. But my shop was still chugging along.

Now if you're in business for yourself these same rules apply. You may not have as many stats to keep though. You might just have stats for gross income and maybe another for, number of people called each day, say if you are and independent insurance sales person. But you would still apply the condition formulas to them.

So managing by statistic is really valuable. Flying by the seat of your pants might seem like fun, but can be dangerous.

Chapter 5

Find and Keep Sending out Great Advertising

Most business need to advertise. This is how you communicate with potential customers. Sometimes people get lucky. They come up with a unique product, put up a web site and the money just flows in. The web site is their only advertising expense. You see them sometimes on that TV show The Shark Tank.

But for most businesses, it isn't that way. You have to find what works for your type of business. You may have to try different things, and that's why keeping statistics is so important. You have to know what's working. Large companies know this and that's why they always ask how you found them. That information is extremely valuable. If you don't ask your customers, at least pay attention, as many will tell you how they found you. They may mention they found you in the phone book or on Yelp, or another company recommended you.

One person selling Herbalife put a sign up at a lake in her home town. When people would go to the lake they think about how their bodies look in a bathing suit. They see the weight loss sign and it worked.

One other person was an overweight executive at a large company with lots of employees. He lost a lot of weight with the same product and all the employees saw this and wanted to know what he did. So he had a built in customer base and sold a ton of product and signed up so many people under him that he quite his executive position to do Herbalife full time. But unfortunately, for the employees he signed up, they were not going to have the same success. Because he already cleaned out the company, they were going to have to find a way of advertising that works for them. Once you run out of friends, relatives or employees, then what? That's why most home base businesses fail.

Now a smart thing to try, which I never did, is to find some overweight person in an executive position in a large company, and give him the product to try. Once he loses weight, you sign him up for all the orders that are going to come in. If that works, find someone else in another company and so on. That would only work by the way, if the product actually worked and the person you found took it regularly and taken properly, Herbalife did work for losing weight. If you try this technique and it works don't forget who your daddy is.

There are some simple things that anyone can do though. Just go door to door or car to car and leave your advertisement. That will work to, but it requires you actually doing it regularly every day. It's brutal but it will work, if you just get up and do it. Of course do it in a city that has people with money to spend.

Your business name

Before we get into the various ways to advertise, find a good name for your business because that's a very important part of your advertising.

Usually short is best. Something that says what you do or are about. I always wanted to irritate my old college friend Larry Miller, of Sit and Sleep fame, by calling my TV shop, Sit and Watch. One hamburger stand in Burbank was called, "Not a Burger Stand."

The building had always been some kind of burger stand, so when I saw that sign, I thought it had become a private resident and they put that name on the sign to keep people from bothering them. They're no longer in business.

Another local limo service is, Music Express. Their name doesn't really say what they do. I thought they just worked for the music industry, although they serviced a lot of accounts in the entertainment industry, the name kind of limits what they do. And by the time they had to shorten it to be on their personalized license plates it became just "Music." It turns out, they originally were a messenger service delivering records and contracts for the music industry.

But whatever you come up with, survey it with lots of people first, I can't stress that enough. Other people may see something in it that's not apparent to you. I named by first business after one of my art pieces, *Frodies Place*, some people thought it was a bar.

Your Email Address

And while at it, keep your email address short and easy to remember. Often you would use the name of your business or the name of the product you sell, but if your business name is too long, it makes it difficult for your customers to remember. And you'll be spending more time on the phone or the internet every time you have to tell it to someone or write it out. I messed up a little on my current one, **czappasstudio@gmail.com**. Not only should it have been shorter, but I always have to explain that there are two S's in the middle. I didn't realize that till it was too late, now I'm stuck with it. Once you have it out there and have it on promotional material and you have given your business card out, it's going to be hard to change it. You may lose contacts if you do change it.

Pick a phone number too that's easy to remember and duplicate. ARC TV is 818-848-9998 And don't forget to put your phone and email address on your building and on your vehicle signs. Another reason to keep it short.

At the same time come up with a great logo. You can pay to have one done or just look around and find something you like for ideas. Keep in mind it should be easy to read and understand and again, follow the laws of communication. And don't copy someone else's logo, it may be copyrighted. On a recent TV show someone came up with something interesting but when you looked close it looked like the Nazi symbol. There have been lots of signs posted on Facebook that told a different story than the person who made the sign, was trying to convey.

I had a printer make some business cards for me and in his sample book there was a logo I liked. I didn't know that it wasn't his and was copyrighted. I guess he figured, it's just a business card, what are the odds that this electrician company, that owned it, would ever know. But I liked it so much I put it on the service truck, on the sign on the building and even in the phone book ads. Then one day while driving in Glendale, I see my logo on the truck next to me.
Soon after that I get a letter from their attorney demanding I remove it. So I had to remove them all and come up with my own design. I changed it enough to satisfy their attorney. By the way, the reason I liked it so much was it looked like a hand pointing, so it called a lot of attention to the name of my store.

If you own, or your landlord allows you to paint your building, usually you would keep it in tune with your neighbors colors. There also may be local restrictions on what color you can use. But for some types of business's, though, it might lend itself to vibrant colors. So keep you neighbors in mind if possible.

Sometimes a mural can be an asset but check with your city first, it might not be allowed, or there may be size restrictions. For a time, in Burbank, they were illegal but in my home city of Venus Ca, they were revered.

But if you do paint your building, do not not spray paint it. Spray paint is used for a shinny flat surface. So when you spray paint a stucco building, it makes any imperfections stand out. Whereas, a roller, stipples the paint and tends to cover up the imperfections. I can always tell a building that's been sprayed. I don't know why people think it's faster, you have to put tarps everywhere and tape up all the windows and awnings. For the inside of your building, for smother surfaces, the paint pad is great. If you're carful you don't even need to use a tarp on the floor with this type of brush.

The different kinds of advertising

Keep in mind that people are more likely to look at certain types of ads then others. For instance, people are more likely to open a sealed, hand addressed stamped envelope than a machine labeled, bulk rate envelope. They are more likely to read mail addressed to them, than mail sent by bulk email. But there are costs involved. Some things cost more but work better. And by the way, pink is the color people will most likely respond to in a flyer

Types of advertising

There are different types of advertising and they have different purposes. Some are used to keep your customers, like a newsletter and other types are there to get new customers. It's important to know this because if you only do one type you may be losing lots of money by ignoring the other types. I never relied on one type of advertising.

So, I'll list some of the various types of advertising and what the purpose is. Remember some will work better for one type of a business and may do little for another type of business.

So what will work for your business will require you to do some research and some trial an error to see what will pull in customers. This should show up as an increase in your gross income stat. Look at your own mail and email or Facebook ads for ideas. Here are some advertising types that every business should consider and some ideas that worked for my business that might trigger some ideas of your own.

Your own web site

The most important thing to have today is your own web site. Your web site is there to pull in new customers and to help your present customers find out things they may not know about your business, like hours your open, or new products or services you sell.

There are also some rules for Web sites too. First keep it simple, you can do all kinds of fancy things today, but they may not work on some browsers. If you can purchase things directly from your web site, make sure it works and works simply.

Try to avoid making people go from page to page to page. And make sure it's complete. I tried to submit work to an art gallery and spent a lot of time trying to figure out how, only to finally find out, they don't accept submitted work on line. How about telling people that! This is also an area to have several people try to use the site and even try to order something. Even if this was made by a web page service, make sure it works and works on the most used browsers too.

I had my home page changed to rotate several photos of my business repeated over and over. I later discovered that my web site couldn't handle that feature. So my web designer moved it to his web hosting site. But if you access it from some search engines the pictures still don't rotate and don't even appear.

The type of web site you need is determined by what you need it to do. If you don't need to change things often on your site, a simple web page where you can change things yourself is ideal. I have my art work on Fine Art America. That site is easy to use and upload photos of my art. People can even buy copies, tea shirts, hand bags and even shower curtains with my images on them. They pay me a commission too. That site was;
https://bill-czappa.pixels.com/

The down side was, it's a longer complicated name. So I went to GoDaddy (A domain registering site) and bought this, **czappasart.com** a shorter name and linked it. The other thing is, FAA is only for art work. But there are many others like them that you can find and check out.

My other main Web site for the store, arctv.net, is much harder to use, so I needed to hire someone any time I need to change anything, so I cannot add things myself easily.

I never sold things directly from my site, so I don't know how hard that is to set up, accepting credit cards and such. But first figure out what you want your site to be able to do. If it's too complicated I would consult a web designer to do it for you. It's important that it's done right. But still check it carefully when their done.

News Letters

A news letter can be extremely valuable. A news letter is designed to keep the customers you already have and make sure they know what new service or sales items you are carrying. They also can be used to give them useful information about the field you're in.

Also, many times in my business, people would forget who they used last and I would get phone calls asking if we were the shop that put out the newsletter? They remembered the newsletter but forgot where we were located, or they never came to the shop, as we just did a house call for them. If the newsletter is interesting and includes data they might what to keep, they may keep it and find you that way.

I would always put a funny short story in my newsletter. People would keep them for years, make copies and even send them to other people and even take them camping and read the short story part around the campfire. They became so popular that almost once a day a customer would ask when the next one would be coming out. Occasionally, if I missed sending one out, people would stop by to make sure they were still on the mailing list. (*You can see some examples in the appendix and the short stories I used are for sale*).

When do you send out a news letter?
Since mine always had a funny short story, usually about the holidays or summer vacations, I would send one out before the holidays and another before summer. Because I did at least two a year, and also gave them a thank you letter, whenever we did a job for them (And many would also get the door to door Junk Mail letter), people thought that I put one out every month. For my type of business that would not have been necessary and would be very costly. Remember you can also over do your advertising and cause a break in communication, especially with too many emails.

So if your business is more seasonal, like it's geared for summer, as in swimsuits or a gym or weight loss products, you would send one before summer time, a minimum of 6 weeks.

But you can also put one out when ever things are slowing down. Anytime you see your gross income starting to fall, get one out. My customers looked forward to the Holiday letter. Some businesses slump during certain times of the year, so if yours does, you want to send one before that season arrives. Tax time can be slow for most businesses accept accountants of course.

The thank you letter.

A thank you letter (sent out to anyone who has just used your service within a week to thirty days or so), is not only to let your customers know about everything else you do, but reminds them that they only have so many days guarantee on any parts or items they purchased. You want them to tell you if something is wrong before the parts or labor warranty runs out. Because, after that point, someone is going to eat it on the cost of the part or item you sold. And you don't want to be the you who eats it.

And you don't want them to give you a bad review on the internet. The last thing you want is to have an unhappy customer that doesn't mention it to you. So, that letter also encourages them to communicate with you so any problems can be handled. I would also include a funny short story in this letter to prepare them for the news letter short story that would be coming later and just to give them something back for using our service.

Some stores give a discount coupon with this letter. I didn't because if they were happy with our service, I new they would come back anyway. I probably would have offered one though, if we were purely a retail store, because that might make them come back to buy a different product right away.

I would have a thousand or more of these letters printed up and stuffed in envelopes ready to go every week, then just print a label, stick it on and a stamp and mail it out. Very effective.

If you collect everyones emails, you can also send it that way for free, but keep in mind, for most people that won't be as effective. Because there is nothing to keep. Especially if you offer a discount coupon, although they could just print it, most people won't. If it gets lost in their email file it will never be seen again.

When people get a hard copy, they hold it for awhile, then they see it again when the go through their mail to through it out. So you get two chances.

The Junk Mail Letter or Flyer.

A Junk Mail letter, (A letter or flyer usually delivered door to door) is designed to find new customers. There's a lot of data out there about this kind of advertising. For instance, this works great for pizza joints with a special discount on it. It works because so many people have pizza at least every two weeks or so. But for my TV service business, where you might not need that service maybe every two years, it has to be done differently, you need them to keep your card or flyer for a long time, how do you do that?

We started advertising with just a small pink 5"x7" card with a house call special on it delivered door to door (*You can see a copy in the appendix*). The reason was it was small enough to keep, or stick on the refrigerator. It always had a discount on it. I would never do a day glow flyer, because it's too big and cumbersome for people to keep. And a business card is too small to put a discount on and too easy to lose.

I also learned that (by survey) it takes, on the average, 6 weeks for someone to decide to respond to an advertisement. So if you put a short deadline you may be wasting your money. In my business it might take them so long to need the discount that I put on it, "Good for ever or to the end of time." I actually got them back sometimes 12 years later. So this has to be designed around your type of business as to what will work best for you.

I later beefed it up, by adding a letter with all the things we do on it and putting it in an envelope. The envelope said on it, "More Junk Mail." Another said, "More Junk Mail no need to open discard as is."

There was nothing else on the envelope so they had to open it to find out, who would do such a thing?

I delivered it by putting it in the Penny Saver Magazine, (*A small throw away newspaper that went out weekly, now out of business*) This was a great way to deliver them because they were sure to be delivered. You could not always count on door to door delivery services putting them all out. So check your own mail for companies like the Penny saver that let you stuff things in their paper.

And because they were in an envelope, people would pick them out, ignoring all the day glow flyers that other companies would stuff in there. And what are you thinking when you're going through your mail? "Junk mail Junk mail," then you see one that says "Junk Mail" on it, it duplicates what you're thinking, you laugh and pick it out and open it up.

I later realized that people need a reason to repair things, so I wrote a letter about that subject, Why Fix things (*You can read it in the appendix*). I put that on the back of the junk mail letter that said all the things we do and put it in the Junk Mail envelope. And that worked really well. Because I was listening to what my customers were telling me, I new lots of people where asking themselves that same question.

I later put this in a window envelope so I could save money on printing costs. In this pack I also put that very effective pink card special we started with, because they would most likely toss the letter but keep the card. I actually had many people call me after reading the "Why fix things letter," and say they agreed with it, but didn't need anything repaired right now, but would keep the card.

And one last thing about giving a discount. People won't believe you if the discount is too high. No one will believe you are offering a 25% discount. Maybe if you're going out of business and have a sign on the business saying you're going out of business, then they might believe it. One competitor gave a $20.00 discount on any repair, but the card said, "You must tell us up front." Well, that just means to me that they're going to raise the price $20.00 "then" take off the $20.00. My special for repairing a TV or doing a home service call was $7.00. That seemed just about right for that service and it was believable. One employee tried to advertise, on the side, and offered $20.00 off, it didn't work. He lowered it to $7.00 and got plenty of work.

When do you put this type of advertising out? These should go out on a regular basis, depending on the size of your business. I would buy at least 30,000 of these or more, because you get a better price in quantity, then send them out over a period of several months. Because they were put in the Penny Saver newspaper, you would have to do at least a whole zip coed and zip coeds varied from 7000 to 12000 homes.

If you're a business selling expensive items, You can also purchase mailing lists. The good thing about them is you can target people and cities who most likely would use your product. But you have to pay bulk rate mail, a lot more expensive, than to have them delivered.

Sometimes, when things got slow, I might have one of my employees go put them out the old way on porches. I found that they were a lot more effective though when mailed. If you do put any flyer out it's illegal to put them in or on a mail box. If you do you will get calls. In fact occasionally we would get a call from someone complaining that we put it in their mail box because it didn't have a stamp on it. Once the post office called as someone complained to them. But we simply explained it was stuffed in the Penny Saver.

Signs on your building and trucks

If your business is in a brick and mortar building, you want your signage to follow the laws of design. Some signs become famous but can be very costly. You'll have to decide what works for you and your budget. Normally you should not have too much signage and in some cities there are laws about how much space you can use on your building.

In my TV repair shop, I followed the rules as far as the roof signs went but, we had large wrap around windows and you could legally do anything you wanted there, except put a sign or banner on the outside of the window. Be sure to check with your city to see what's legal.

I put way too many signs in the window because we did so many different things. And we were located right next to a very popular health food market with lots of foot traffic. And we were across the street from another very popular handy market. So those signs pulled in a lot of customers. In the largest window I would put some of my newest artworks.

Since I housed my art work in my shop, it was also my personal art gallery. You're not supposed to mix two different businesses, but sometimes violating the rules works. People would come in to see the art and we would end up with a TV or tape duplication customer. Some of the art was made from old TV sets. And because it looked so interesting inside the shop we ended up renting the place for several TV shows and a Disney movie.

For signs on your vehicles, just look around at other signs, see what ones you like. Now that they can print signs on vinyl, and just stick them on, people have been getting too fancy, in my opinion, to the point that you can no longer actually read the sign. Don't make it so fancy you can't read it. The message is what's important.

Having something catchy is not a bad idea, depending on the type of business you're in. . I put a line on my sign that said, "Life happens when your TV breaks." It didn't work, only three people ever mentioned noticing it. I should have surveyed it more. But a really good caption can go a long way. And your logo on your employees cloths creates a professional atmosphere.

Phone book adds.

People do use phone books today, usually older people or poorer people who don't have a computer or are not on the internet or have a cell phone. So if your business caters to that group of people, consider at least putting a listing in the phone book.

My business did cater to a lot of seniors but we also did a lot of different things, so we had to be in a lot of different categories. But in the end, before I sold the business, I would only pay for listings in the different categories we needed to be in. I no longer had to pay for a large ads. In some categories we would be the only listing, which was great! Most phone book companies will give you one free listing in the category of your choice.

And one tip, always avoid signing up for auto renewal. Make them contact you when the next contract if due. And, a lot of them will try to charge you for digital charges, that's their on line phone book. I never would sign up for that because who would go there? Most people just Google what they want or go directly to your web site or Yelp.

Free web sites Yelp and Google

Besides having your own well done website, Yelp and Google, will give you a web page and you should always claim these free pages and put up some photos of the shop, hours of operation or products you make and hours of operation etc. You can also put a discount coupon and that will also help to let you know how they found you.

These sites are also great for getting new customers. And they usually pull in a good quality customers, because people trust other peoples recommendations, so those customers are often easier to deal with.

That is, if you have good reviews, which is the reason for the thank you letter, so you can handle any complaints before they give you a bad review.

Yelp and Google paid for advertising

This is used to find new customers. If you have great reviews you can also link it on your web site. You can also pay for advertising on Yelp. How the plan works that my shop tried was, when someone searches for businesses that does what you do, an icon appears on their Yelp page that says, "You might also consider." I'm not sure what they would do if you were the only one in town doing that service though, so keep that in mind.

With the plan we tried, Yelp charges for every one that clicks on one of your ads on these pages, so if you have lots of bad reviews that can be a waste of money. There are other plans too, so check with them on those.

Also keep in mind that if you happen to be in a business with little competition, you may be getting calls from far away, out of your service area. That could be a plus if you are just shipping things, but if you're doing service calls that may not be worth your time. Even though you tell them, 5 miles, you may get calls from much further because it's in Yelps best interest to get as many clicks as possible. Apparently Google also has similar plans, check with them if interested.

Facebook Ads, Tweets and Instagram

You should also open a Facebook page for your business. You can then direct your customers to go there through your newsletter or thank you letter and friend you. Then whenever you have something new to offer, or have a sale, you can reach them all. They also offer an option to boost any post. Then it will go to lots of new people on Facebook. I tried doing a "boost your post" ad a few times for my art work, but didn't do a thing for me.

Tweets are good too and Instagram but trying to get people signed up for all these services can be the challenge. So try to keep your address name the same for all of them. And keep in mind some are more appropriate for some kinds of businesses, and may do nothing for others. But they're free, so why not?

TV and radio advertising

This type of advertising can be very expensive and you have to buy it in blocks to be effective and to get it cheap enough. This type is for larger companies with huge budgets and is very effective if done right.

There are companies like Alan Mendalson, who gathers up several small businesses and has a ½ hour TV show each week. I only got one customer out of it, but it was inexpensive and I got a well made commercial that I then put on my web site. I did it a second time, with another company, and I didn't get even one call but I got a second commercial for my web site. (*You can go to my web site to see them arctv.net*). I also did a radio commercial that played numerous times but it only got us one customer.

One time one of our famous customers, Bill Blake, called in to the Tech Guy radio show with Leo, Laporte. He gave us a great review of our business, and while he was talking, Leo pulled up our web page so anyone watching him on line could see it.

We instantly got phone calls and emails. Unfortunately most were from San Diego or out of town, so it didn't do us much good. Accept one person showed up and sold us some vintage TV sets which we needed for rental to the movie industry.

If you want to see that episode it was #1414 , 19 Aug 1917). I reposted it on YouTube and should have put it on my web page too.

YouTube

This is a new and exciting way to advertise for some types of businesses. Before I realized you could make money on a YouTube posting someone else got me to make a few videos about cleaning the heads on your VCR etc. 64,000 people had a look, but no leads, because the guy putting it up didn't even mention my shop.

Since then I did put up videos of some of my art works, One has 1400 views but I have not made a single sale from this site. A videographer did a really well made video short of the shop and my art, it went viral on Vimeo, because it became a staff pick, 34,000 people saw it, but not one sale. National Geographic also put it on their web site, another 5,000 people saw it, not one sale.

These can be a great place to market the right business though, particularly if you do it as a weekly blog and keep it up. You can get a huge following and sell a lot of product that way. There are books on how to do this and how to do it best. Check it out if that sounds right for your business.

Craig's list

This is a great site to sell items and services. It worked great for us renting our vintage TV sets to the movie industry. Most categories are free, but you have to remember to keep reposting your add. It did not do anything for selling my art. It's great for finding things you may need for you business. I did use it to find employees though.

EBay

EBay is great for getting rid of excess product. Part of my business was for posting things for other people who are not computer savvy. One year I sold $25,000 dollars worth of base guitars and a B7 organ for one customer. I also got a hold of 40,000 very commonly use diodes. It took a year to move them all in batches of 10 and 50, but I did really well on those. Also great for finding things you may need for your business.

You can also offer services there too. For us it would have been video tape duplication, for instance. But the other people offering that service, made it not worth our time. But it might be great place to explore, for the right product or service.

Fax or email advertising

This might be good for a home based business to find new customers. You buy a email or fax mailing list and send out your ad. I used fax mailing once, before there was much email, to sell Herbalife. But when we ran out of local places to fax we tried San Francisco and ended up with a $300.00 phone bill for that month. So you may just want to stick to emails lists.

It can be quite valuable to have the emails of your customers. But the problem is many people have long and difficult email addresses, so unless they emailed you and you saved it, and I always did, getting them written down by hand accurately was always problem. Even when I had the customer write it down, sometimes you still couldn't read their handwriting.

A great way to pay for advertising?

And how did I pay for all this advertising? I found Itex. It's a trade organization where you trade your service or product with other members who're also in the system. Itex is one of the oldest trade groups. For a 10% cash charge to Itex, on everything you buy or sell, you could sell your wears and then use those credits to buy things you may need, like printing. There is also $30.00 monthly fee paid out of your Itex account and a yearly fee as well.

There are also other trade services. They wanted me to be in another one, but I found they all had the same members, so that was a waste of money paying monthly fees to both.

Besides paying for advertising, I got my first computer on Itex, rented a place to stay in Hawaii, got my vehicles repaired, dental work, acupuncture and even a case of wine one time. The local newspaper was on trade too and just being a member made you available to everyone else in the system.

Surprisingly, often they had a better price than people who were not in the system. It was like being in an exclusive club. People would stay in it for years. Some new people would come in and not get it or try to over charge to make up for the 10% fee. They usually don't stay long. So the 10% cash charge is really just an advertising expense.

At times I had $20.000.00 in my Itex account. I found a printer and another company, that was also on Itex, that would stuff and seal the envelopes. And much later found an even better company, *We Mail for You*, that would print the envelopes and newsletter, stuff them, label them and even mail them out. Now all we had to do was send them the copy and the mailing list, via email, and that was that. At the end we had 14,000 people on our mailing list.

As it got larger we would divide it up. And as customers returned for service, we would put them at the top of the list. Thus, if we later didn't want to do the whole list, we would be hitting the most active people. Although it's a good idea to mail to the oldest people on the list as well, sometimes, because you never know who might become active again. And they may not know you now offer new services or products. So if you're buying an existing business, the mailing list is one of the most valuable assets.

Frodies Place, my first business 1970

Chapter 6

Always Give Customers More Than They Paid For

When you're in business you're exchanging your service or product to your customer for money or trade. Most businesses give you a dollars worth of product or service for a dollar worth of goods. That would be even exchange. You get what you paid for.

Criminal exchange is this, you pay for something and get less or nothing at all back. But the best kind of exchange is giving a little more than your customer paid for. That can be things as simple as carrying their item to the car for them, giving them a free bag to put there item in or what we did, sending a thank you letter with a funny short story and then later a newsletter with some good information. Doing a little more will guarantee you success.

The worst thing you can do is give even exchange and then screw something up. If that happens you are heading for criminal exchange. You prevent that by having good training and keeping up the quality of your product or service and by being professional.

And if you mess up, taking care of the problem somehow. The person who ran our local 99 cent store lost power in there building. She was standing out front handing out cards that gave everyone a free product.

Being professional is a worthy goal. It means that you conduct your work in such a way that it's worth paying for as opposed to an amateur just helping out in some fashion.

Giving more than they paid for can include being professional. Not wasting their time because you forgot a tool or forgot to do some procedure or pay a bill on time. Not leaking oil on their drive way.

One plumbing company advertises, "The Smell Good Plumber." I have never got that close to a plumber or had one that stunk up the place, but that would be a good thing to not do. I recently had an attractive teller at the market who's breath was so bad I could smell it across the counter.

So think about what you can do for your customers that's giving them a little bit more than they expect.

Chapter 7

Find and Keep Great Employees

If your business needs employees, that can be the most challenging thing to handle, you will need to learn a few things about being an employer. There are all kinds of people out there and some are great and others not so much. These days it has gotten harder to check people out before you hire them. You should know this before doing an interview or even posting an ad that there are things you can and should not ask. You can look these up on line for the state you live in.

If you call the businesses they listed as references, in California anyway, they only have to tell you the dates they worked there and if they would hire them back again. That's something to go on because if they have lots of jobs, in a short period of time, or the company would not hire them back, that could be a bad indicator.

In California you can also ask for their drivers license print out. First, that guarantees they have an active drivers license but can tell you a lot if they have had many violations or even too many parking tickets. In other states be sure you check first to make sure it's legal to ask for this data.

If they're going to drive for you, it's a good idea to have your insurance company do the checking as it's almost mandatory that they have that data anyway. One time I asked a potential employee for this and he called me back later saying, "I have to take care of something so I can't work for you for awhile."

Larger companies can afford to make potential employees go to a employee screening company that evaluates them. They give them a battery of tests including drug tests. This can be costly but can save you a lot of time and money over all.
There are places that find employees for you too, head hunters. I never used them because the ones I checked out charged a lot to find someone. Not something a small company can usually afford.

But when you really get down to it, you really have to try them out. I would always tell them there is a three week trial period before they would be permanently hired. And after all, they may not like working for you either.

If you get lucky and find a good employee make sure you do what you can to keep them because they're hard to find. You know they're good because you have put them on stats and their stats are consistently high.

One of my best employees, Raul, had a handicap from Viet Nam, but he came to work for me, took over one post, got that in, then took on another area, got that in and soon he has handling most of the front office. He had very good communication skills and even the people we ordered parts from where complementing our shop because he always stayed in good communication with them, treated them with respect and never gave them static.

So take care of those kinds of employees and don't work them to death. If you are a larger company you can give some of their less important tasks to someone else, so they can produce more on the more important tasks they're good at. In other words you give them assistance so they can produce more and not get burnt out.

Another great employee Lloyd, was our bench repair tech for 17 years. Sometimes units would come back for some reason. Either they had an intermittent problem or something new happened. Lloyd would check those units first. And that's a great thing to do because, that's when your company really shines, when you have to take care of a problem.

The other thing I noticed is some people have the ability to "Intend Work." Lloyd was one of those people. Whenever he would take a vacation, he would finish up all his current jobs and work would stop flowing in. Then a few days before he would come back, it would flow in again. Some people have that ability, it's a metaphysical thing, but those kinds of employees are very valuable, their like magnets.

I have had employees get snippy with customers who brought something back, That's the time to be extra nice to them.

And one last thing, don't pay people every other week, that may make things easier for the company but is a crappy thing to do to your employees.

So find then, nurture them and keep them.

Real Power! *1987*

Chapter 8

Weed out Antagonistic Employees

Over the years I realized that there is one type of employee that you get a lot of, I call them Antagonistic Employees. They're ones that cannot follow the most reasonable instructions. It isn't that they can't remember, much worse than that, they are intentionally not following orders. One indicator is, they have to do everything their way, which is usually the wrong way. It's as if they are working against you and have to either overtly argue with everything you ask them to do, or just quietly not do what you asked. And you had better understand that they <u>are</u> working against you.

Interestingly, they can also be the owner of a company too. They'll even destroy their own business. One of them bought one of my business from me and did just that (See chapter 14). You see them sometimes on those TV shows like the *Profit* or *Kitchen Nightmares*, those shows that try to help failing businesses. They argue with any reasonable new idea the host comes up with and usually, after the show ends, they go back to their old ways and often go out of business anyway.

I should have known with one of these types, his bumper sticker said, "Don't get mad, Get even." I thought of even putting this on my application for new employees. I was going to put a list of sayings and have them check off the ones they like.

That could be very reveling. If you detect this type of person it's a good idea to get rid of them as they're not there to help you at all and can cost you money and time lost. If you find you're working for one of these types I would quit. Any great new ideas you have will be squashed.

Monument to the end of time   2012

Chapter 9

Have Great Training and Lots of It.

The best thing you can do for your business, and for your employees, is have great training in place. And have lots of it. Training in communication, as I mentioned earlier, is the most important thing to get in, especially with people who have to talk to the public.

But the better you grove people in the smoother your operation will be and the more happy your customers will be. Well trained staff impresses people, it make them think your operation is professional and cuts down on communication breaks. It also creates high moral for your staff because they feel they are working in a professional environment and working as a team.

I had all my posts written up. So you could just sit the person down who was taking over that post and let them read it. For the counter person, I would have them read the post write up, then have them find things related to that post, like the various price lists, were receipts were kept, etc. It also contained an example of a properly made out invoice. Then I would drill them finding a customer's receipts as if a customer had just showed up to pick their unit. So you get the idea, every step of their job you go over and drill till they got it. After that, you would work with them as customers came in and handle any errors as they came up.

So you get the idea, drill it into them that there's a standard way to do things and to do it some other way, screws everything up. And when training people this way, just handle one thing at a time, don't overwhelm them with too much data too fast. A lesson I had to learn.

For an outside technician or delivery person, I would first go on a test drive with him, to see how good of a driver they were on our large van. You don't just hand him the keys. You might want to wear a helmet. One employee nearly ran over a pedestrian, then when we parked, he didn't put the truck in park and it began to roll into the street. Another employee, had three minor accidents in one month's time.

If he passes that test then I'd have him go to the service truck and open up every caddy, so he knows where all the tools and common parts are. After that I would have them go on several house calls with me to show them the standard way of doing them.

Now after they are on post for a few days, there may be some errors, just handle them as they come up and make him read the policy that covers that over again if necessary.

And today, I have noticed there are a lot more people who have memory issues. That is deadly because if they cannot duplicate your training, and especially your policies, you will be getting lots of problems.

I did some research on this and discovered energy drinks and too much marijuana can cause memory issues. I'm not a prude, you have no idea how much marijuana I stuffed up this nose. But, do what you want with that data.

School of Hard Knots   *2017*

Chapter 10

Write Good Polices and Make them Known

Polices are usually written because you had a problem and you don't want that problem to happen again. If you leave the barn door open the chickens will get out, so don't leave the door open. Sometimes polices like that end up as a sign posted on the barn door. If your staff doesn't know the polices of the business, you will be getting all those problems again that those polices where put there to prevent.

That should be part of the training for new employees, drilling and getting in all the polices his post will be dealing with. And if you're buying a company, be sure to have them tell you about all the polices that they have learned and they may not have bothered to have written them down. You may have to drag them out of them.

Sometimes you find a company that has some policies that just don't make any sense. It might just be some quirk the owner has. I went to an Italian restaurant that only served wine in an old glass jam jar instead of a wine glass. I guess they thought it was quant, but for me it ruined the oviance of having a glass of wine.

Chapter 11

Be Able to Take Advice and Listen to people

Being able to listen to people and accept advice is a valuable quality to have. Some people have to do everything their way and in fact, sometimes you see people who will do just the opposite of what you suggest (As mentioned in the chapter on Antagonistic Employees). They will do this even to the point of harming their business or their own interests. If you bought this book you are most likely not one of those types of people.

This is so important that you may have noticed that large companies often ask people to do a survey so they know how they're doing. Unfortunately some of those surveys are multiple choice and miss the item that I didn't like and would love to tell them about. So if you do a survey, make sure they have a place to leave a comment.

But you can learn a great deal by listening to others. Your customers will tell you what they like and don't like about your business. I wouldn't ever say the customer is always right, I don't even know what that actually means, but they should be listened to, (*It probably means, don't make them wrong and cause a communication break*).

But, customers can give you some valuable information, from how they found your business to, if they think your prices are fair.

This also includes to listening to your employees too. One new employee worked for a business that rented, delivered and set up audio video equipment to hotels and banquet rooms. He suggested I get into that business too. I sent him to our local Holiday Inn, (*That we were already repairing all their TV sets for*), to see if they were interested.   They were interested. Luckily for us, they didn't like the company that they were using, who didn't know the rules, and we were in. A whole new money making branch of our business was formed.

Carpenters Lament   *1992*

Chapter 12

Have Your Accounting in Order

An important part of any business is having your accounting and records in order. This can be easier today than ever before, due to the computer. For payroll we now have QuickBooks. Although when it comes to sending in your quarterly payments Form 940, 941 and DE88, I could never could get it to add things up perfectly. So I still had to have a bookkeeper check the figures before sending them in.

If you are large enough you may have a bookkeeper on post. But whatever you do, I would encourage you to learn enough about all the things the bookkeeper does. Especially if they are also in charge of assets. Willie Nelson learned that lesson the hard way, he relied on a major corporation, Price Waterhouse, to handle his investments and they messed up. Willie ended up losing everything including his home and even, his awards.

Now you wouldn't expect Willie to go and learn all about finances, investments and book keeping, but he could and should have hired someone else to go over what the other company was doing.

The point is, this is an area where you should be on your toes and don't fully trust anyone (Bernie Madhoff).

The other area that it's important to have in order is your receipts. It's just bad form to not be able to find a work order to see if something is still under warranty or what was actually done. You could always insist the customer show you their copy of receipt, but to do that is bad form and creates a break in communication. One major big box company sells a lot of extended warranties. They count on the fact that most people forget they bought one.

TV's and VCRs started failing sooner and sooner and if everyone remembered they had purchased an extended warranty, and used it, that would have put this company out of business. But even though, I'm sure they had a record of these sales in their computer, they insisted the customer show them their paperwork or they wouldn't honor the warranty. Which makes a good point about your records, if you're not going to have neatly labeled file folders, at least throw every receipt in a box. It might take you awhile to find an important receipt you need someday, but at least you'll have it.

And don't forget to back up your computer. One of our fellow business's had all their records in their computer. Receivables, inventory, employee records, all of it. Their computer man was doing backups, but no one ever checked to see if they were any good. They had to spend hours and hours of time to re-enter all those records.

There are now cloud services where you can send your data and have it safely put somewhere else. Don't just rely on one service though either, with all the data failures, don't just trust one back method, put it on a disc.

And don't forget to keep your back up discs at a different location than your computer, in case of a fire.

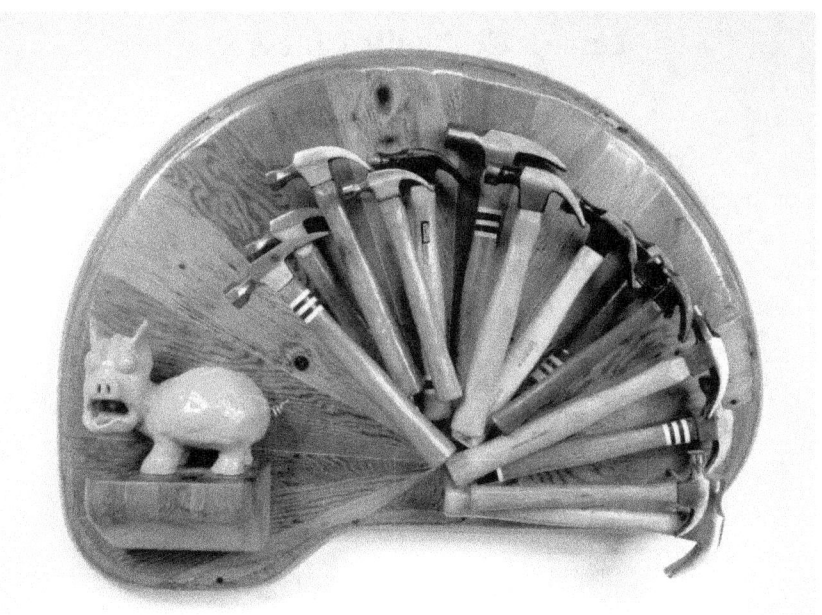

A Pigs Interest   *1991*

Chapter 13

Run an Ethical Business

Always make sure you and your staff are running your business in an ethical manor. Being ethical guarantees that your business is being run safely. To not follow the law leaves you open to risk, loss, penalties and bad reviews. Make sure you have all the necessary licenses and permits in order. Put in writing the agreements you make with your employees.

Good contracts make for good employees and customers. If you're paying commissions, put it in writing in detail so your employees know what to expect.

I just went to a new dentist and the person who gives you the estimate, I told verbally what I wanted. Just a cleaning and the cheap crown. But when I saw the document she had me sign, all in insurance coed, I realized she was over selling the job. After confirming this with my insurance company, I realized she had blatantly lied to my face. So I complained to their corporate office and demanded a refund for the service I did not agree to. If it's not handled they will be getting a charge back, visit to small claims court and certainly a bad review on Yelp.

Being ethical also includes keeping your word. Not promising things you cannot deliver.

Today if you do things that are unethical it can be know pretty quickly due to Yelp and Google's reviews. But there is also a metaphysical reason that I have observed. I hired a TV tech who was ignoring some of the harder jobs. He wanted the easy work but those jobs stopped coming in. But instead of getting the hard jobs done he just sat there waiting for the easy stuff.

But the rest of the store was extremely busy, so it wasn't just a dip in the economy that can happen. But soon as I got him out of there, and finished those back logged jobs, TV's started flowing in again.

I tried to explain this to another VCR tech who would do the same thing. His finances were in such bad shape that I had to pay him every day so he could pay his bills. But he would put the hard jobs aside. Then he would do an all-nighter and get caught up and work would flow in again. After observing this several times he finally agreed with me that it was true.

There is also a less than metaphysical reason this happens too, If people call and ask how long will it take till they get their unit back, if the person on the phone knows that department is back logged, that is going to come across in his voice if he doesn't out right say, "They're back logged so could take longer than normal."

Occasionally someone would add the bill up incorrectly. My bookkeeping program would always find those kinds of errors. And I would immediately refund the amount that was in error. When you do things like that people know you're an honest operation.

Chapter 14

Real life Example of What <u>Not</u> to Do

This is an example of how to destroy a business in just a year and a half. By ignoring most of the rules I wrote, you can see how one person wrecked one of the businesses I sold. I'll call the new owner Joe. The first thing Joe did was start "organizing things." Now he had been a TV repairman but many of the things we did he had not done before, like microwave ovens and installing TV antennas. I stayed on and gave him two months training as part of the deal and after that worked for him for 3 more months. But he really didn't take the time to find out how the business was set up and how it ran before he started messing it all up and changing things. He didn't go on enough service calls with me and ended up yanking a microwave off the wall destroying it in the process because he didn't know how that model came out.

I had one service caddy in the truck for servicing TV's, microwaves and stereos and another caddy for installing TVs on walls and to install microwave ovens. I also had a pouch that had all the tools needed to mount TV antennas and re-route cable lines.

By the time Joe was done, "organizing" he had 5 caddies in the truck and none of them complete. He didn't like the service caddy I used because it was "too heavy." So, better to go on a house call and carry in 3 or 4 caddies instead, all of them adding up to the same weight. Or run back and forth to the service truck for a tool or part that's in the other caddy.

But not being fully trained on some of the things we do, he left many specialized tools and parts in my caddy which was now back at the shop. Which meant that he would eventually find himself on a service call and have to drive back to the shop to get that tool or part.

And true to Murphy's law, that would be a service call that was the furthest away from the shop and you could only get to it by the busiest and slowest freeway in LA.

Then, he didn't like the two sided pegboard racks that held most of the common parts and belts we used every week. On some of the most common ones, I had a sticker that had the part number on it so you wouldn't have to look that up every time you wanted to reorder that part. What does Joe do? He dumps all those parts in a couple of boxes. He at least doesn't mix the transistors with the belts, but he doesn't separate the flat belts from the round belts from the large ones from the small ones. Now if you need a belt you have to look through a box with 100 belts in it to try and find the one you need. That's a costly mistake if you're paying people hourly and you end up buying stock that you may already have but can't find.

He needed to order new receipts with his new business license number on them. I Suggested he start with the number one because we were into 5 digit numbers by then and it's easier to find a ticket if the number is smaller. But no, Joe couldn't do that either. He starts with 5 digit numbers.

Now on advertising, instead of continuing what was working and had kept us in business for so long, as our competitors died off, he only uses Yelp. When you take over a business it's a great idea to, at the very least, tell your customers that you are taking over and will be continuing the business in the same manor. Otherwise people show up and everything is different and they're going to be confused. At least put a sign in the window saying, "Under new management." Although, you should <u>defiantly</u> do that if the guy you bought out had a bad reputation and not as helpful if the guy was great. However to let them know what's happening keeps them informed and more likely to use your service again rather then start all over with someone new. In other words you stay in <u>communication</u> with them.

Now his Yelp advertising did start working, at first. Although it was hard to tell because of our great reviews, Yelp brought us a lot of work anyway. But the problem became this, for Yelp advertising to work you have to keep your reviews positive and he didn't do that. And he didn't even answer the bad reviews which just made them worse.

Although he got some really great ones too, the numerous and viciousness of the bad ones, meant that he could not advertise that way anymore. Because you would be paying people to come and read your bad reviews.

I also discovered that one of his competitors on Yelp was a guy who repaired everything in the home, because he didn't have a shop. In the TV repair business everyone wants things done in the home. Somehow they think they can't be cheated or it will be faster our they can watch you and make sure you do a good job. None of that is true. I've followed many unscrupulous shops cheating people right under their noses and doing shabby work. Sometimes you may need to order one part, then you install that part, only to find out there is something else up the line that is also bad and you have to then go back again with that part. But if it's in the shop, you don't have to bother the customer over and over again. You also can test it, or burn it in, and make sure it doesn't have an intermittent problem and again not waste the customers time or your time. Often today you sometimes can only get rebuilt parts that are not as tested as they should be. And you can always solder a circuit board up better sitting comfortably on a well lit service bench rather than crouched on your knee's on the floor. I've seen techs put in the wrong part that was just close enough because they didn't want to drive back to the shop for the right one.

So when you have a competitor like that, you don't want people to go to Yelp. That's the purpose of your newsletter or your junk mail letter for new customers. You want to get them "before" the other guy who is pretending to offer something better.

A year after selling the shop it was going under just like all my competitors. He couldn't use Yelp anymore and even if you don't buy advertising on Yelp, they'll pull in a lot of customers for free if your reviews are good. But he didn't want to do what has always worked and was now thinking that things "suddenly had changed." No, the thing that changed was not doing the advertising that worked! The advertising reminds people that repairing things is **still an option!**

I couldn't even get him to hand each customer a flyer after each repair telling them everything else he did. That always brought people back for some other service.

Then he took the advertising off the service truck. Why would you do that? When you go on a service call your customer's neighbors see who their neighbors used. Not to mention your truck is a traveling bill board. When I worked for Ham the Zenith man, he had a 4x8 sign on his trucks in day glow letters. If we had a two man pick up, he would always send both trucks out because of the advertising. He wanted people to think we had a fleet of trucks. Companies actually pay for advertising on vehicles now.

There was vine growing on the outside of the building but the faucet started leaking and instead of taking care of it right away, it leaked for two weeks, the flower bed got soaked and killed the vine. It's now dead, brown and falling off the building.

Then, they put a new roof on the building. The roofers, not knowing these rules either, didn't put the sign back up correctly so it's now slanted and crocked. And there was an America flag up their too that is now just threads. So the outside of the building looks tattered and shabby (see photo). There's also a huge window that I always had some art work in. I suggested he at least put some of the vintage TV sets in the window that he rents out. That would at least be aesthetic and pull people in because they would be curious.

That's why the film and music industry rented vintage TVs from us because people like to see them. But no, he just put one small led TV set in the window with no explanation (Is it for sale is it for rent?) wasting all that great advertising space. The huge spider that took up residence there was interesting though.

Joe then had a problem with the company that pays us for scrap TV sets. So they stopped picking them up. Now the shop was filling up with used TVs blocking the isles and spilling out into the parking lot. He stored some of them in back of the shop and his neighbors business and even poked holes in her screen. Customers now were having trouble entering the parking lot. And now it looked like he was running some kind of a junk store.

And in just the first two months, he caused a break in communication with all the employees and they all left. He hired two new ones and he did the same thing and those two left too. I stopped by one day and he was working by himself, had the air-conditioning off because he couldn't afford to turn it on any more.

So you can learn a lot from this. First, when taking over a business you must gather up all the lines, all the procedures, all the little things that make the place run. **You do not change anything at first** unless some area is in an <u>emergency condition</u> of some sort. My next chapter is a list of all the areas you need to pay attention to when taking over an existing business or if you are a new manager taking over a division of a business.

Once you get your feet wet and have it running, don't change anything if the business was doing good. Keep doing what the last owner did. Then, and only then, you can do a pilot program on some area that you think you can improve on, say advertising. You might try something new and see if it works, but don't stop doing what has always worked in the past.

There may be procedures that could be improved in the operation. Making things flow better. But make sure you know why it's the way it is first.

There could be a good reason for them doing it that way. Listen and ask questions of the staff if they were there before you bought the place. Often they know what improvements would help things run better.

ARC TV and art Gallery 2016

ARC TV September 2019

Chapter 15

Check List if you're Taking over an Existing Business

This is a check list that covers most of the areas that you have to cover when taking over a post or a business. Often people don't write down these things and once the owner is gone you'll have to wing it. And for the person selling a business, it's a good idea to write this all up for the new owner to because if you don't, he will be calling you every day and forever.

And I would suggest never ever taking paper or payments for a business. It's also a bad idea to let them work there <u>before</u> they buy the place, that's a sure fire way to lose a sale. Because it's hard to take over and it can be overwhelming at first and if they're not fully committed, it's easy to give up.

This is just a general list, as each item may have several parts to it. I've also tried to put it in the order of the most important.

1. Get papers signed with the landlord. This is the first thing to do before Handing over any money, make sure the rent won't go through the roof or the landlord isn't about to sell the building.
2. Are there business or trade licenses that are needed?
3. Is there any monthly bills that you will have to pay? Like monthly phone book adds?

4. Sign up with board of equalization, edd & U.S. Treasury.
5. Get vehicle insurance, workman's comp. etc.
6. Change owners ship of vehicles or rental equipment.
7. If you're buying their receivables, get the paper work for them.
8. Sign up for a credit card service
9. Transfer any email and internet services.
10. Payroll, what program or service do they use?
11. Payroll, who gets paid what and when?
12. Transfer over the utilities and phone lines.
13. Banking, what bank are they using?
14. Who are the venders they use? Phone # address's and what ones are preferred for what products or services?
15. Phone numbers and addresses of everyone needed.
16. Open accounts with these vendors.
17. List of items they keep in stock and who they buy them from and how many.
18. Complete inventory list.
19. Companies that they advertise with.
20. Copies of advertising that worked and didn't work.
21. Companies they may rent equipment or space from.
22. People they use for troubleshooting computers or equipment.
23. Charts that show their trends, gross income etc.
24. Get their regular customers phone, mailing and or email list.

Appendix 1

This is a letter I wrote to get new customers put in our Junk Mail advertising. To write a letter like this for your business, give them the reason they would use your business or your product or why yours is better than using someone's else's.

Why fix things?

I have been in the consumer electronic repair business since 1969 but only in the last few years have I noticed that I am being asked this one question now several times a day, "Should I fix it or buy a new one?" With the advent of cheap home electronics, VCRs, TV sets, stereos, and now even printers, fax machines and microwave ovens, people want to know what to do when their equipment breaks. " To fix or not to fix," that is the question? Their dilemma is only compounded by the prevalence of cheap replacements on the market.

Well, at a time when we are being asked to separate our garbage for recycling, why are manufacturers urging us to just throw away that old TV monitor or VCR -- not recycle it but dump it in the nearest landfill? Just throw it away, even though it is full of toxic material, including lead, and other toxic stuff? Are the manufacturers actually urging us to just dump it, even though special precautions are now made (at huge expense) to get lead paint off of a house and have it carefully dumped in special toxic control sites? Not to mention there is now an added mandatory toxic fee charged on new TVs and monitors.

Besides the toxic issues, just consider for a moment all of the wasted energy and resources that go into making any of these products. Metals, plastics, IC chips, PC boards -- all made using our resources and energy. Not to mention the Styrofoam, cardboard, and fuel necessary to ship it, usually from Mexico or China. All to deliver you a poorly made product that now lasts only one or two years, and all too often, only six months. Then, you, as a consumer, are given the privilege to drive down to your local discount store and start all over again. Wasting more resources to acquire another product that may not last as long as the one you just tossed.

The quality of new products has been dropping for over 10 years now. Most products today only last 2 years or less before needing repair compared to ten years for products made a decade ago. When people discover this, they often mention the TV or VCR in the bedroom that lasted 15 years. This is because some of the best quality products were made in the 1980s.In the 1990s, as Wall Street thinking started driving the economy, quality went out the window.

Welcome to the New World economy, driven by "the bottom line" to deliver you a poor quality item so some Wall Street stockholder can have a higher dividend on his investment.

About 30% of all TVs and stereos just need to have their circuit boards properly soldered. The reason they come un-soldered because the manufacturers are now making the circuit boards by putting parts on both sides of the circuit board so that they will not have to drill as many holes. Because of this, they can no longer dip the circuit board in solder as they used to do or they will destroy the parts they put on the bottom. Instead, they are sprinkling the board with a poor quality solder dust and melting it with a type of blow dryer device. The connections come un-soldered in just 2 years instead of lasting 10 or more years like they used to do.

This is all done in order to bring you that cheap TV, although this same poor way of soldering is done on the more expensive models, too, so they don't last much longer than the cheap ones. This problem is readily repairable by soldering the broken connections by hand with the proper solder; the way circuit boards should be soldered. When done properly, your product can easily last 3 times longer than when it first left the factory.

The second most common defect is, the manufacturers often put in a few undersized or low quality key parts, which promptly fail. Once these flawed parts are replaced with a quality part, your machine can last longer the second time around, sometimes by many years. We are actually in the business of re-manufacturing electronic equipment when you get down to it.

And consider this, another 60% of all broken VCRs, CD players, DVDs, fax machines and printers are not broken at all but just need a good cleaning and nothing more. What is the solution to all this? Don't give up on your equipment so quickly. Have it checked by a competent repair person first. Spare our environment from more toxic waste. And, as most electronic manufacturers are now foreign-owned, taking your money out of the country, investing in a repair is good for our "local" economy. Save yourself some money, too. It is often the cheaper option because our American ingenuity can make it better and last longer, saving you money and energy in the long run.

The End   **William Czappa**

Appendix ll

This is an example of the 4"x6"pink card that we inserted into the news letter.

VCR or DVD
Heads / laser
Cleaning special
$27.50
This card is good for one Professional head Cleaning on any VHS VCR brought to our Store. Also good for DVD, Camcorders & CD laser cleaning. This is an $11.00 savings Off our regular price. Head and laser Cleaning is always free with any major or minor repair.

2529 W. Magnolia Burbank, Ca. 91505

This card is
 Good forever.
Or the end of time!

(818) 848-9998

Appendix lll

This was our flyer for new customers. The other side would have our letter, "Why Fix things."

More Junk Mail

Yes, it's more junk mail but what the heck, how are we going to let our neighbors know we are here and ready to service their TVs, VCRs and Camcorders or sell them new or rebuilt equipment if we don't say something?

Anyway, if you don't already have a reliable TV or VCR service man, give us a try. We are the TV store of choice of NBC Studios and have been servicing Disney, Warner brothers and many other businesses and over 12,000 of your neighbors since 1965. In fact we have repaired over 40,000 units since 1983 alone.

We have fully qualified expert technicians who are factory trained. So we can provide expert service faster and for less money than most factory service centers charge. And in spite of what Circuit City salesmen say it is almost always cheaper to repair than replace. Our techs can repair Camcorders and Big screen TVs the right way. And by the way, properly cleaned mirrors and lenses on a Big screen TV can add over 30 percent to its brightness and clarity, have you ever had yours cleaned?

If you are in the market for a new TV, VCR or Camcorder, come and see us first as not only do we have very competitive prices; we can clue you in to which companies are selling dogs. And a dog TV or VCR will bark all the way to the repair shop.

And if you are tired of paying high cable rates consider having us repair or install a new antenna for you. TV reception is free and most areas can get all of the lower broadcast channels 2 thru 13 plus many UHF channels for a tenth of the cost of those ever increasing cable rates.

So let us know if we can be of service to you. Your inquiries are always welcome. Please look over the complete list of services and sales items below to see if there is anything you need or want and visit our web site for more data. If you don't need anything now save the pink discount card for later.

SERVICES:

Televisions All makes and models serviced. We make home service calls or you carry in and save even more. We also repair remote controls.

Big screen TVs We have expert service on Projection TVs, all makes. We clean mirrors and lenses.

VCR'S All makes and models serviced, including 3/4". Installation and operations explained.

Stereos AM/FM, CD's, Cassette & speakers. Phonographs are our specialty.

Antennas VHF, UHF, and FM antennas sold, serviced and installed. Cable line extensions and repair.

Camcorders We have expert techs who can repair your camcorder fast and the right way.

Microwave Ovens All makes and models serviced we do built-ins too. Apartment management accounts.

Computers & Monitors We repair computers, Laser and regular printers and monitors. Fax machines serviced too, all makes.

Film Transfers Transfer your 8-mm home movies to video. Audio and video tape duplicating. We also repair broken audio and videotapes.

SALES:
New Units TV, VCR and Camcorder sales (Zenith, Panasonic, Hitachi, Goldstar and many more).Competitively priced. We can probably beat anyone's prices on Big screen TVs and Camcorders. Industrial and broadcast quality TV's, VCR's, camcorders and editing Equipment.

Reconditioned Quality reconditioned TV, VCRs, stereos, CD, cassettes and more. Fully guaranteed and at great prices. Ask us why our used equipment is better than new

Attachments TV antennas and parts, VCR hook-up cables, VCR Plus, blank videotapes, tape re-winders, camcorder accessories, tripods & batteries

RENTALS:
A/V Rentals Overhead projectors, 35mm slide and 16mm audio projectors, TVs, VCRs and Big screens. TV, VCR   Microphones, amps, stereos and others. Camcorders Weekend, weekly, daily and monthly rentals.

**(818) 848-9998 * 2529 W. Magnolia Blvd. *
Burbank, California 91505
Home page: http://www.relaypoint.net/~arctv**

Appendix IV

This is our thirty day thank you letter mailed to every customer that bought something. This would let them know of all the other services we offered. On the reverse side we would put a one page short story to get them used to seeing them. It was called a thirty day letter because we would mail it within 30 days of them picking up their unit or order.

"The Service, Rental and Sales People"

Dear Customer,

We want to thank you for using our store recently, whether for a repair, rental, purchase or tape duplication. It was for a repair or sale item we hope all is well with it. If there is something wrong, please don't hesitate to let us know. We want everyone to be happy with our repair and sale items. Please don't wait until the warranty is up to get it checked out, especially camcorders. Remember most parts we install are guaranteed 90 days and labor on what we repair is 30 days.

Also, a lot of people don't realize the extent of the services we offer. Besides repairing TVs, VCRs and other electronics, we also service microwave Ovens, stereos, phonographs, cassettes, CDs and much more. We also rent all kinds of equipment, from camcorders to microphones, amplifiers and speakers for sale and training seminars and Big screen TVs for those major sporting events! And we duplicate and repair both audio and videocassette tapes.

So thanks again for your time and please look over the list below to see if there is anything else we can help you with.

If you don't see it just ask and please visit our home page too.

TVs & Plasma, LCD   All sizes, makes and models of TVs. Big screen and projection TVs. We do home service calls or bring it in and save. We offer pickup and delivery at a nominal charge too. We also install Plasma and LCD TV sets on walls.

VCRs & DVDs   All makes including 3/4" professional machines and time lapse. From head cleaning to a full rebuilding, our service is fast and efficient. One day DVD & VCR cleaning.

Stereo & Audio   All makes and models serviced. CDs, cassettes, tuners & amps. We also specialize in repairing record players and tube amps too. We fix speakers and answering machines.

Microwaves   We repair all makes and models of microwave ovens and do house calls on built-ins.

Computers & Printers   We repair Computers, printers, and laser printers and fax machines.

Antennas & HDTV   We repair and install antennas, repair and run cable lines, and hook up TVs, VCRs, stereos and surround sound systems. We are HDTV antenna experts.

Sales New and Used   We sell new and rebuilt TVs, VCRs, and stereo equipment. We are a Zenith, LG, Toshiba, Mitsubishi dealer and sell, Pioneer and many other makes. Check our prices on Plasma and LCD HDTV's. Our prices are competitive with the Big guys and our equipment is more often newer and fresher.

Audio & Video We rent, slide, 16mm film and overhead projectors. Video projectors, Big screen TVs,
Rentals DVDs, VCRs Camcorders, Plasma and LCD TVs.

Tape Duplication We make copies of tapes, even European and copies of your old 8mm or 16mm movies film to tape or DVD. They make great gifts. We also make audio copies to and from CD Phono and reel to reel.

Lamps & Small We fix lamps of all sorts, toasters, hair dryers, curling irons, phones and many others

Appliances Odd items - just call and ask, we once repaired a bird incubator.

eBay Posting We post items you want to sell on eBay for you from electronics to antiques. Our service includes photographing, packing & shipping. Call us for pricing and details. We purchase to.

Recycling We are an approved electronic waste recycling drop off center. Safe recycling at no charge. TVs, printers, lamps, stereo, DVDs and most other electronic waste accepted.

Art We are the oldest art gallery in Burbank showing the internationally sold California Assemblage Sculptures of Bill Czappa. Web site:
www.czappa.com
ARC TV & VCR, 2529 W. Magnolia, Burbank, CA 91505 Phone: (818) 848-9998

Appendix V

This is one of the 1page short stores we would put on back of our 30 day letter listing all the things we do. Write your own or you can purchase them from me, these are all tried and true.

Baseball

I don't know. Suddenly, it just hit me. I'm not sure if it was this summer and the Fourth of July that triggered it, or what. But there it was, just like that, right out of the blue, like a bolt of lightning! I was starting to *like* baseball.

Well, I don't mean that I would actually go to a game or anything, or listen to it on the radio or read about it in the newspapers, but just the same, I was beginning to just, well, *like* it.

I always liked that other people like it. It's just so American. I mean, I always felt better knowing that other people enjoyed it and what would summer be without it anyway? It would be a summer without flies, watermelon or cold beer. Not always in that order, however.

This all started on my first real job. I made gloves for my aunt and uncle for a dollar an hour. That's when a dollar was worth a dollar-- not a dollar twenty or fifty-two cents, but "exactly" one dollar. They had a little store right across from the Helms Bakery building on Venice Boulevard. It was called the "Banneck Glove Company." That was when Helms was still making donuts and bread. I guess they stopped making donuts 'cause they stopped making bread.

Well, I worked in the back room, just me and a six hundred degree boiler pressing gloves over a very hot metal hand, thinking of surfing and my girlfriend, but not always in that order. And in the other room was the thud sound of my Uncle cutting leather with a mallet and next to him was my aunt on her sewing machine, sewing up those pieces of leather into gloves.

But in between those sounds was the haunting sound of Vince Scully on the radio calling out the plays. And in between all that clamor was my aunt yelling back at the radio, cussing out Drysdale. She'd say, "Why the hell they leave him in so long? He's only good for five innings! Why the hell they leave him in?"

Well, someone else would get a hit off him and she'd be at it again. This time a little louder, "Damn it, why the hell they leave him in, he's no damn good." Then she'd light up another cigarette and uncle Casey's mallet would thud down one more time, and I'd press one more glove and summer would just creep on by like that, mallet by mallet, glove by glove, cigarette by cigarette, and play by play.

Well, I liked that. I mean, I really like that they liked baseball but I had other things to think about, like surfing and my girlfriend, but not always in that order.

And these days, I'll think about that girlfriend and surfing but I like baseball just a little bit more, not that I would actually go to a game or anything, or listen to it on the radio or read about it in the newspaper. I just sort of *like it* a little bit more.

The End   **William Czappa**

Appendix VI

This is an example of our full newsletter and a Christmas story. It always had a short story, newsletter with tips about TVs, microwave ovens or TV reception etc. and all the things we do on the last page.

An RCA Hollywood Christmas !

I was thinking about the holidays this year and my thoughts wandered back to one of my very first jobs with a major corporation. In fact, come to think of it, that was the only job I had with a major corporation. It was the RCA Color TV service company in Hollywood California.

This was probably the best and easiest job anyone could ever have, probably as easy as being president or the head of General Motors. One of those cushy jobs you never forget and will never ever find again. Now my cohorts in this story were Charlie Muir and Paul Scott. Charlie was not only a Fraternity brother but also a schoolmate going back to Daniel Webster Junior High. We both took Electricity 101 together with Mr. Payton and it was there that we learned (in just 3 painful weeks) how to strip the insulation off of a piece of wire real, real good. Paul and I went all the way back to Betsy Ross grade school in Culver City where we learned how to daydream and look at girls real, real good. It was Charlie who first got a job at RCA and then recommended Paul and me for a position as "Color" TV repair technicians.

Now back then color was king. This was before computers and if you could fix a "Color" TV, you were the man. Of course when computers came around many TV techs learned how to fix them too just to amuse themselves.

There were so many aspects to this job at RCA that were great. Like, we had to drive a long distance to get there, which gave us the opportunity to ride our motorcycles to work each day. When you ride a bike to work, the further away it is, the better. Except or course, when it rained or was just too darn cold (as it often got as we approached the Holidays). Then we would take my 1953 Buick Special instead. It's funny, now come to think of it, the 53 Buick was a hand-me-down from my father which he drove to work too, down that very same street years earlier. He took Venice Blvd. to downtown and I would veer off to Hollywood. Yes, "Hollywood," tinsel town, tuff town, my town.

Now I remember the shop executives at RCA wanting us to pick up our service calls from the Dispatcher and to get on the road as fast as possible each day. I remember rushing into work along with all the other techs and stopping by Rosie's desk.

Along with her regular duties (which I never could quiet figured out what they were), ran the coffee and donuts concession each day. Rosie would diligently collect our dimes and nickels, which would be used to pay for the annual Christmas party at some swank hotel. Well, to 19-year-old boys, that sounded like a deal. To have coffee and donuts and then get to go to an office party with all the cute secretaries? We would have been glad to pay a lot more for those darn donuts.

As I said, we all rushed in, got our calls, and then rushed out just as fast. Most of the techs just rushed right down the street to the coffee shop where they proceeded to have a real breakfast. That is, a real long, long breakfast (like 4 hours long).

You see, a good tech would get 8 service calls a day and you could usually knock them off in about 3 hours, unless they gave you a picture tube job to do, then it could take 3 ½ hours. They really didn't want you to come back for more calls, as there would not be enough for the next day. I tried to once. Sandy, the dispatcher, just said, "Why don't you go and have yourself a nice cup of coffee." That was the longest 3-hour cup of coffee I ever had.

This was a union shop, but unlike the well-paid unions, like the United Autoworkers Union, for instance, we got paid crap. But, hidden in our paltry benefits, we did get a light workload. In fact they could have fired half the techs and then there would have been just enough work for everyone left.

Well, I was not one for sitting around chewing the fat for hours each day, so I decided to use my time more wisely and, well, build a boat. As everyone else headed off for the coffee shop I rushed out to do all my service calls and then head back to Culver City, by noon, to work on my cruiser. Paul Scott's mom agreed to let me use her garage and driveway to build it, not realizing how large it was going to be. She was thinking "row boat" and I was thinking "Cabin Cruiser."

My intention was to build this ship and live on it in the newly built Marina Del Ray boat harbor. I also intended on having lots of bikini clad babes on board as often as possible to. I didn't actually know how to get bikini-clad babes aboard yet, but I did know how to build an ocean going vessel. And I was sure that if I did that, the bikini-clad babes would soon follow.

Now in order to pull this off I was going to have to get my calls done really fast. I had the Beverly Hills-Hollywood route and often some of those calls were way up on top of the hills overlooking Hollywood.

So, I got to be a pretty good driver and only got one ticket the whole time I worked there. But, one day the manager, "Sid Callen" called all us techs in for a shop meeting and proceeded to describe what he had seen a few days earlier. He said, "I walked out of the building a few days ago and I noticed one of our service trucks coming around the corner…on two wheels?

It then proceeded to almost run me down, then turned the other corner, … "on two wheels," and then entered the back lot coming to a screeching stop. As he described this event I realized that among these 30 or so techs present he was actually talking about me! I had delivered a TV set, but forgotten the remote, and in my hurry to get done (and most important back to the boat for some more "boat building") created the as-for mentioned incident.

It was almost as bad as the "special" meeting called because Charley Muir's truck had, let's say, become a trash dump! He often would have a late afternoon snack of KFC or Pioneer Chicken and would never bother to throw anything out. The truck just continued to fill up with chicken bones, skin, boxes and wrappers. Well, it was as high as the seat and reached all the way to the back of the van. I mean he really loved his chicken. I must admit it was a lot to handle in the hot summer months. But as we approached the chilly Holiday weather, which had a tendency to keep the decomposition process and gasses down to a minimum, it was really nothing to much to mention.

So, Charley could not understand what all the fuss was about. He saw nothing wrong with chicken bones and wrappers falling out of the door every time he got in or out. He of course also worked the swank, litter free, chicken bone deprived, homes of Beverly Hills.

Now, Paul was no angel either. He rushed out to the local coffee shop one morning leaving his tools back at the shop. He had to go back to the shop to retrieve them in order to make his first service call of the day at around 3:30!

We could never understand why the managers just didn't come up and talk to us personally. They always had to have a whole "shop meeting" to tell us. It never did make sense but that's what corporations do. Thinking back, it was probably the Chicken Delight dinners they would buy us to eat after each meeting that made them call so many meetings. Union rules maybe? I don't know. I never found out.

So that's how my days went. Fixing TVs really fast, building the boat, and then hurrying back to the shop to check in. I'm not sure how many extra miles I put on that service truck or how much gas was wasted driving back to Culver City, but it must have been substantial. Things got even better working there just after Thanksgiving when a new secretary was hired and I couldn't keep my eyes off of her. After that, no matter what direction I went, there was something beautiful to see, "my boat" or back to work to see the "secretary."

She was the kind of girl that the other techs would kid about. They would make comments about her, they'd say, "She's, look, but don't touch." I thought, though, that she was just a little shy like me and I like that a lot. She was a little on the short side and I liked that too.

She had the greenest eyes I had ever seen and the cutest pouty-est lips. Lips that said, "These could be yours, just figure me out." Each day as I turned in my receipts to the cashier I would smile at her from across the office, she would smile back, and I would try to figure her out. The only thing I figured out though was her name, it was Marlene.

But, I was painfully shy and she was painfully beautiful. I had visions of her being my date for the shop Christmas party that was coming up soon. Then one day, as I returned from the field, she was standing by the back door and I actually mustered the courage to ask her out, although my question sounded more like a plea or casual remark or flippant comment and well, she said no. If she had said yes, I would have probably passed out. I was actually kind of relieved.

As we got near the holidays I took my mind off that incident by noticing how nice the homes I was going into, now decorated, looked. I even got to work on Dean Martins TV set. He was not home that day but his son was, (the one that died in the air force a few years ago). He was playing a drum set that was set up in the foray of the house. The foray was so large I thought I could put my whole boat inside of it. In fact I thought that, "This would be a great place to build my boat." I could put my table saw over there where the drum set is and move the kid up to his room. Dino could come down once and awhile and sing Valero while I worked. But how do I get it out the front door? I still do this when I go into anyone's house I figure out how I would arrange things, let's see, the Bar over here and the bikini clad babes over there.

Well, we finally arrived at the long awaited "Christmas Party" and everyone looked fine all dressed up in suits and ties.

The only thing reminding me that these guys were actually TV techs, were all the bald heads and well, the great jokes. I don't know why that is but there is an alarming number of TV techs that are bald. In fact one night, at the annual obligatory union meeting, the glare off all those baldheads sitting in that auditorium was blinding (the jokes weren't all that bad either).

Now, even though I was only nineteen, and since we were in a private room, I thought I might be able to have a real drink. Un-fortunately, after being asked for my Id at the bar, I had to ask for a coke instead. When I turned to go to my seat, Marlene was standing behind me taking it all in. I watched from my seat as I saw her buy a "real" drink and then it suddenly sunk in, she was 3 years older than me. It was not to be then nor later, I had been seeking an older woman and didn't know it. Charley thought it showed some balls though and was quiet impressed that I had even attempted to ask her out.

Soon after the holidays our union, The United Electronics and Feather Workers of America, went on strike or more accurately (to illustrate how bad our union was) we went on strike against our union and RCA. So, I realized, I may never see Marlene again. After the strike most of us techs realized we could make a lot more money, let me rephrase that, "a hell of a lot more money," not being in the union and many of us never went back.

Then one day, years later, after marrying and having moved to the San Fernando Valley, I ran into Marlene.
There she was working in the office of a jewelry store sitting behind a typewriter as I always remembered her. And there I was holding my newborn daughter, but somehow I could not look at her, I knew it was her and I knew she saw me but I didn't look her way again.

I thought a lot about that afterwards. I thought this could have been her child I was holding. And years later when I had divorced the woman who bore that child, I thought, maybe if it had been her instead that would not have happened.

Maybe it would have been different. We were only three years apart. What's three years in all of eternity? Just maybe, I would be going home to her for the holidays this year, that nymph of a secretary with her green eyes and pouty smile. Who knows, maybe things would have been spelled and punctuated a little better around here two.

The end   **Bill Czappa**

2004   **ARC TV Gazette**   **Circulation 10,000**
++

Well once again we hope you enjoyed our newest True Hollywood story and if any of you are getting duplicates or just don't like to receive mail, just let us know and we will be happy to take you off of the mailing list. Just call, email, write or leave a message on our machine. We have now over 10,000 people on our mailing list.

The full version of this story is also on the internet site with a few photos from Paul Scott showing the back of the RCA Service lot in Hollywood circa 1969 and me building my boat in his mothers driveway.

If you would like to read more of our stories or purchase a booklet of 36 of them they are still on sale at the shop for only $5.95. And if you are in the neighborhood stop in and see the new work in our art gallery.

You know ARC TV is also the oldest art gallery in Burbank now going on 21 years old. It was in the San Fernando Valley art tour this year.

Also if you are online visit our Web site as it has been recently redone with many new items we service or sale and twice the number of art works on display as well.

We now have our own web master working for us and so we have also ventured out into web design. If you need a whole site created or just a few items changed John is the one who can do it. We have continued to upgrade our tape duplicating equipment and can now handle more duplications and in even more formats as well, from your old home 8mm film movies to a simple VHS copy to DVD.

Now on to some tips that may save you money on repairs of your electronics.
Monster cables, at a monster price to pay.
Many people are spending huge sums on Monster cables to hook up their equipment.

I have seen people pay more for their cables than the DVD they are hooking them up to. It is really not necessary to use expensive cables to hook your DVD or VCR to your TV or surround sound system. I defy anyone to show me the difference in picture quality.

Although the Monster brand is made very well most TV's, VCR's and DVDs "aren't." People are breaking the RCA plugs right off their units when they try to take off a Monster cable. In other words we have reached the point where the cable to hook it up is built better than the thing being hooked up! To prevent this do not just pull a Monster cable off. Instead gently twist it as you pull.

And while on the subject, as the manufactures continue to produce crap the RF fitting on your TV and VCR is no longer put on very well either. They used to be soldered on. But no more time for that, they have money to make. My god you know what solder costs? Well, actually hardly anything. Go figure. I was going to make a joke saying that if they make things any worse the buttons will be falling off then realized that we just had several Sharp

Microwaves come in where the buttons did fall off. They were only six months old!
On camcorders.
Camcorders more than ever are very delicate devices and as such do not hold up well with sand in them or water either. So, when going somewhere dusty, windy or wet take the time to at least rap your unit in a clear plastic bag with rubber bands. You can do so in such a way as to not block the lens on most units and still operate the controls and see the viewfinder.
 They also do not like extreme cold or heat. And why anyone would think smaller is better.
 These new tiny little palm-camcorders are not made very well. They are extremely fragile. These are not well made items.
HDTV update As predicted by me the date for the changeover to HDTV has been postponed till 2010. So there is no hurry to rush out and buy HDTV. So the pressure is off.

Zenith and LG

Zenith now has offered a second line of TV's called LG. So don't be confused if you start hearing about this new line it is not new it is Zenith and we just signed up to be a new LG distributor.

All The Things We Do

TVs All sizes, makes and models of TVs. Big screen and projection TVs. We do home service calls or bring it in and save. We offer pickup and delivery at a nominal charge to.
VCRs & DVDs All makes including 3/4" professional machines..

Camcorders time lapse. From head cleaning to a full rebuilding, our service is fast and efficient. We offer one-hour head cleaning on request. We service all makes of camcorders VHS, 8 MM, Digital 8, Mini DV and even digital still cameras.

Stereo & Audio All makes and models serviced. CDs, cassettes, tuners and amps. We also specialize in repairing record players. We fix speakers and answering machines, too.

Microwaves We repair all makes and models of microwave ovens, too, and do house calls on built-ins.

Printers & Monitors We repair Computers, printers, laser printers, computer monitors and fax machines.

Computers We now can build a whole web site for you are just change a few pages call for more info.

Antennas & HDTV We repair and install antennas, repair and run inside cable lines, and hook up TVs, VCRs, stereos and surround sound systems. We are the HDTV antenna experts.

Sales New and Used We sell new and rebuilt TVs, VCRs, and stereo equipment. We are a Zenith Dealer and sell Panasonic, Quasar, Toshiba, Pioneer and many other makes. Check our prices on Big screen TVs and HDTV. Our prices <u>are</u> competitive with the big guys and our equipment is more often is newer.

Audio & Video We rent Video, Slide, 16mm film and overhead

Rentals projectors. Big screen TVs, Camcorders,

Amps mics, flip charts and more for weddings, parties and sales-training meetings.

Tape copies We make copies of tapes (most formats, even European) and copies of your home movies. We also make audio CDs from cassette or reel to reel.

Duplicating 8mm or 16mm movie film, too. They make great gifts. We also make audio copies to Cassette or CD.

Lamps small We fix lamps of all sorts, toasters, hair dryers and other odd things to

Appendix VII

Other examples of short stories I wrote for the newsletter, and just to give you a little bit more. This one could be used anytime as it's not seasonal.

Finding Ginger

I think its important to mention that sometimes my stories are made up or embellished but I have to say this one is an entirely true story. It took place just after the holidays and I was at a friend's house for a party. I was showing off one of my new artworks there and we were having a few drinks.

Well, all was going fine till this girl walks in the room and our eyes met, well more like locked. She was my ideal idea of a woman. Her tight, short, silky, lacy, frilly, black dress left nothing to the imagination. Her curves were all in the right places and exactly the right size. Her clothes seemed to be enjoying themselves. She looked like a mixture of Fergie from the Black Eyed Peas, Carmen Electra, Sherilyn Fenn from the movie, Boxing Helena, and several girls I had known in college. She was one of those girls a little on the short side, not bony, that had a little baby fat. She also had fantastic green eyes. I tried to make the perfect woman once with Photoshop. I scanned in those three women together but when I was done it looked like Betty White.

I asked a friend who she was and he said, "That's Ginger, she's getting divorced." Well as the evening progressed she seemed to be well attended but I couldn't help notice her furtive glances and eventually I ended up talking to her. She was fascinated with the artwork I had brought.

As we talked I could tell we would become an item. She said she loved how the work, not only gave off smoke and had moving parts, but she really loved my creative use of pasta.

Later I ended up in another room of the house and discovered my friend Brian was concerned that we had been spending too much time together. It was apparent he was very interested in her as well. I said, "Brian, aren't you happily married?" He said, "But just look at her." There was another guy following her to with that lustful look in his eye. I asked who he was and Brian said "Oh that's her brother."

As Ginger came back in the room I then became aware that every guy in the room was looking at her, even Tipper and he was gay. As the party continued Ginger and I kept trying to find a place to be alone. We walked casually from room to room chatting but every room we went through guys were hoping to have some time with her and their girlfriends or wives seemed to be annoyed.

We finally found a secluded place in the foyer and she said, "I am sorry about that" (meaning all the attention from the other guys), "I'm a bit of a flirt. But I think there is something very special about you." She said this while looking deep in my eyes and I just grabbed her and kissed her deep and long.

We then held each other and she started to lick my ear. I wanted to kiss her again but she just kept it up. Then suddenly I woke up, my dog Muffin was licking me trying to wake me up as I was late.

As I drove to my studio I couldn't help thinking how real this dream was. I couldn't get her out of my mind.

A week went by and then I got a call from a collector, he said he wanted to see my work and I set up an appointment for him to come in.

I said, "How about Thursday?" Thursday's always a good day for an appointment, it's not the beginning of the week and if it goes bad you have Friday and the weekend to get over it.

He arrived and with him was his wife, Ginger. She was the girl I had just dreamed about. He introduced me to her and I shook her hand, but she held my hand a little longer then was comfortable, since her husband was standing right there. I just couldn't break the stare that we mutually were embracing. I knew it was the girl I had dreamed about and wondered if she knew as well.

He said his wife had seen my work online and wanted to see it and show it to me in person. As I showed him the piece Ginger was most interested in (the one she liked in my dream) she was fondling him but flirting with me in the most obvious manner. She rubbed her hand up and down his arm standing real close and posing. She excitedly told him how the piece produced smoke, had moving parts and she loved the clever use of pasta.

Then she asked to use the ladies room. Jack then said "That was a show just for you, you know. Don't worry though, we're getting divorced. We will always be friends but we can't get along.

The final papers will be signed next week. Somehow she got really interested in you and your work about a week ago; she just can't stop talking about it."

When Ginger returned he told her he was buying the piece for her as a divorce gift. She was ecstatic. He then said, "I have another appointment. Why don't you get to know each other and show her the rest of your work and if you wouldn't mind could you drive her home? We live near here in Toluca Lake." I said I would be glad to and he left. I casually put up the closed sign and turned off the phone.

As I strolled with her around my studio showing her the rest of my work, she put her hand around my arm and stood very close, taking every possible chance to look deep in my eyes with a look that said, "I'm all yours." I finally couldn't take it any longer and just pulled her close to me and gave her a deep long kiss. We embraced and as we did I could smell her hair, but it smelled a little like doggy shampoo. This was confusing but somehow I didn't mind. She began to lick my eyelids. I thought "Well this is interesting," and as she continued to lick them, I woke up. Muffin, my dog, was trying to wake me, as I was late for work.

On the way to the studio I was still thinking of her and as I came to a stoplight. I looked in the Lexus next to me and there she was. She turned; saw me and I could tell she was surprised to see me too. We both knew that what happened, had happened. As the light turned she gave me a little wave and I waved back. Her husband was driving, they turned left and I never saw her again. His license plate read "Woof Woof."

But I could still hear her hot, sultry sexy voice in my head when she described my piece - "I love how it produces smoke, has moving parts, and that ever so clever use of pasta."

The End   **William Czappa**

Antipasta   *2016*

Appendix VIII

This is a great summer story for a newsletter. This is one of the first ones I wrote.

The Barbeque

I don't know if it was now or later that I became aware of the "barbeque" but when it happened is not important, only that it did. So many years and so many steaks and chickens later, I still reflect on those morsels that went before. But in these years, I must say that those years seemed better and indeed they were, since everything is better when you are eight, and it's the Fourth of July.

A month earlier our parents had sent out invitations to all our friends and relatives to come to a "shindig" -- a shindig, they called it. But to me it was the Fourth of July and cousin Carl was going to be there, my ol' buddy, friend and life-long pal. The adventures we had and were to have put Hollywood to shame. But we didn't think or know so then. It was life that showed us the truth.

As the day approached and school ended, I realized that I would not see Peggy (the class sweetheart) again for several months. I thought that I had better turn my attention to something real and reachable, like the Fourth of July, rather than daydream about the impossible Peggy. That was a good idea and one that I wish I kept, but unfortunately lost in later years.

Well, as the weeks passed and the day approached, the arrangements kept piling up in anticipation. I was in charge of the yard. I began watering the lawn daily so that on the final day it would be as green as our '53 Buick. I had planned to cut it the morning in question so that it would have the most profound effect on our guests.

The patio had needed painting and several weeks before my sister, father and myself had gotten all the paint we had on hand and painted each of the scribed imitation flagstone panels a different color: the colors that would reflect the fireworks we already saw in our dreams.

Time grew closer and then suddenly it was the morning of the Fourth and we had lots to do. The brick icebox, my father had built into our patio, had to be washed out and filled with ice, soda and beer and, of course, the lawn, now very green, had to be cut one last time. Our Doughboy pool had to be cleaned and the bugs removed from the surface, and the most fun of all was, the hamburgers had to be made.
This year, my father had made a hamburger press and I couldn't wait to use it. It was made out of wood and two coffee can lids that pressed together. I would lay out two pieces of wax paper with some hamburger in between and presto, it was like magic! Perfect burgers.

The day started like that and went slowly, much more slowly than now. The guests would not arrive till about noon and there was still the long wait till dusk and the fireworks.

Then Carl showed up and the day was complete. My ol' buddy, friend and life-long pal was there. The day could begin. We swam for hours and all the grown-ups joined us with movie cameras whizzing. My father ran and dived in over the side of the pool.

We still have film of that momentous event. Well, all the swimming just made us even more hungry and the burgers began to sizzle over the charcoal grill. The charcoal was not the same either. We didn't have these perfect little cubes like today. No, they were real pieces of charred wood, hard to start, but somehow it was better, more natural than today. Anything real is better as we should all have learned by now.

We ate and ate the corn on the cob, and the potato salad, which I still do not like but am glad that others do, as it seems a necessary and important part of barbeques that maybe someday I will appreciate and perhaps someday will even try again.

Well the party rolled on and me and cousin Carl ate our food sitting in my soup box racer as his father rolled lit cherry bombs under my car to our delight and fear, as we realized they were dangerous, our hands showing small signs of blood.

After more cider and more fun the night began to come, which was necessary to conclude the grand finale of this glorious day.

A day we would remember for all of our lives and would never be repeated again in quiet the same way, no matter how we tried.

And at last, at the very last moment, the most astounding thing happened. My friend, who lived across the street and a few doors up, (just cross the city line) was also enjoying the fourth with his family and relatives, who had bought even more and bigger and better fireworks than we had, came to talk to us. Fireworks were not legal in LA where they lived, so we all agreed that they should bring their party, (and especially their fireworks) to our house in Culver City where God lived and made the laws.

Days earlier my dad had made a special stand to shoot off the "cones," and "pinwheels" on, and as the sun set, in the last moments, the men began to hammer up the final touches to the upcoming display. We had already lit our "worms" and "Smoke Houses" and were beginning to set off our "Sparklers" as the sun finally set.

Then it began. The sun was gone and the first of three hundred and fifty two fireworks we now would share in turn did their thing, and I might add, for a longer period of time then today. And, yes, us kids did count every one of them, several times.

When we ran out of "Piccolo Petes," we would scream them out with our mouths and would be echoed by others blocks away doing the same thing. But the "Pin Wheels" had not yet been torched, nor had the big "Cones" or the "Roman Candles," as the night went on seemingly forever. So much smoke began to float down the street, from others doing what we were doing, it seemed like the city had been fogged in and the air was thick with gun powder and smoke.

Well, I don't remember how that night ended. Perhaps It never did or maybe I still want to savor all the fun we had.

But it does live on in my memories
and I know that someday it will happen again. So I
keep watering the lawn and cleaning the barbeque,
just in case. And I wish I could find some apple cider
that tastes as good.

The End

Appendix IX

Another example of a summer story

A Catalina Christmas

I was nearly 21 when the following incident happened. I was in my third year of a two-year college and living on a boat that I built in Marina Del Rey. Up to that point in my life I had never missed a Christmas with my family and later with my close friends. And so it would be a big deal for me to just ignore the holidays as my parents had instilled in me, as it was something they could not live without. Growing up and helping them over decorate the house and yard each year was something even I looked forward to, even when I was no longer a kid. And I kept up this holiday spirit going probably in an effort to somehow keep my dad's spirit alive after he passed away. So I have always had something to do or somewhere to go for Christmas. I even got a small Christmas tree for my boat.

That's my boat

But this year things had changed; I had just lost my girlfriend Candy Wayne. You know, losing a girl friend just before the holidays is just not the thing to do and looking around I realized my prospects for having close company, family and a holiday feast, something I always enjoyed, were getting pretty lean. And no one was planning to be at the fraternity house either on Christmas day.

Steve Rice invited me to go with him to Las Vegas and stay at his mother's place, but I just had that experience the previous year. We were to fly there, have a fine turkey dinner at a good restaurant and see the town. But unbeknownst to me, once Steve and his mom had a few drinks and started talking, no one was going to go anywhere. So we had Wild Turkey for dinner instead. And to make things worse, they didn't have any mixer.

They were straight drinkers. And so it was pretty sad the day after Christmas when we finally did make it to a restaurant and I ordered turkey. The waitress had this look of pity on her face' but I was a traditionalist and I had to have at least one bite of turkey on Christmas or at least soon after.

So this year, feeling rejected and forlorn, I decided that I would forgo my usual Christmas celebrating for once and see what it was like to spend it all alone for a change. And the most alone place I could think of was Catalina Island in the winter. So it was on that Christmas Eve afternoon, I boarded my boat, a 22-foot cabin cruiser and headed for Catalina Island all by myself.

It was always dangerous to take a small boat out there even with a crew.

I didn't have a marine radio or even flares and cell phones hadn't been invented yet.

There was always just enough gas to get me there and back.

One slight mistake, just ten degrees off course and I would be found deep at sea eaten by penguins. I was even relishing that prospect, that'll really make Candy feel sorry I thought. I hadn't learned yet that the person doing the dumping never gives a thought about you again.

Well, I knew of a somewhat protected cove we had just visited last summer called "Goat Harbor." I would go there. I had aboard turkey helper, cranberry sauce and a can of black olives. I just couldn't give up on all of my holiday traditions you know, those family customs run deep.

Yes, I would go to that bay, throw anchor and have my holiday meal out there alone in the wilderness.

I left early enough to get there before the sun set. The trip up the coast was fine and going across the channel the water was pristine. But I had a ominous feeling, as it was a little too smooth, a little too glassy, especially for a cold winter afternoon. My boat was not a deep V hull made for ocean travel but really a lake boat with a planning hull and on a glassy day like this it got up and rode on top of the water. I got there in no time. But, just after anchoring things changed. The wind came up and the waves became larger. I had to set a second anchor.

I settled down for the night, although settling was not the right word, as the swell were getting bigger by the minute and I found myself in the middle of the night having to make a sea anchor from the canvas from my fish tank. It worked by keeping my bow into the incoming swells but soon after that my camper propane heater gave out and I realized it was going to be a very cold holiday. I put on my sailor cap and got out my best nautical jacket.

I thought back to my friends on shore and wondered what Candy was doing with her new boy friend. She was probably snuggled up against him in front of a warm fire. I found some solace in the fact that she didn't even know where I was or what I was doing.

And somehow that thought made me even more determined to stick it out. There is a small reward for wallowing in self-pity and remorse and the environment I was in was helping with that feeling quite a bit.

Well, I awoke the next day and it was still turbulent but a lot calmer than before. And as the morning wore on I began to realize that an adventure like this was really just not all that fun.

I put on an 8-track tape and the first song that came on was "Sloop John B." "I boarded the sloop John B, my grandfather and me."

And in fact, what was a wonderful bay in the summer time, was a hellhole in winter. It was a lonely and desolate spot to be in. Even the trees on shore looked lonely and forlorn. I thought about why Candy said she had to leave me. She had met another artist whose work spoke to her in ways that mine didn't. She said she just couldn't be with an artist who spent so much time making art out of pasta. She needed to be with a painter or at least a calligrapher. "Pasta," she said, "Would never hang in 'The Louvre,' although it might be served in the cafeteria."

And so as I began to cook my Christmas dinner I turned on the radio and another song came on, Macarthur Park, "Someone left the cake out in the rain…. I don't think that I can take it, it took so long to bake it and I'll never have that recipe again…."

That was it, that song always got to me, I just couldn't take it any longer. I had enough of this. I pulled up all my anchors and headed for home. No matter what loneliness faced me back at the empty frat house it couldn't be any worse than this place and it would at least be warm. That is, soon as I got a bottle of rum and lit me a nice fire, urrr.

The waves in the channel were getting worse by the minute. Some were getting so large that when I went over the crest my propeller would come out of the water. But I had a new determinism and I pushed that ocean going vessel through the waves on the straightest course I could manage,

I didn't want to spend one more minute at sea, I remembered my geometry, the shortest distance between two points was a straight line. And after two agonizing hours and short on fuel I was once again safe in the breakwaters of

Marina Del Ray harbor and heading for my slip. There were penguins on the rocks eyeing me with a menacing look; they had missed out on a fine meal.

I immediately drove to the frat house to dry out, warm up and reminisce about my journey while nursing a beverage.

As I pulled up to the house I could see some people inside and one people was a very attractive young lady with long brown hair sitting in the window. She turned to look at me just as I got out of my 1953 Buick Special, our eyes locked and she gave me a big smile. I thought wow, this looks promising. Inside next to a roaring fire I found Jack Davies, one of my frat brothers. He was there with his girl friend Beverly and she had invited her friend Linda along. Jack immediately offered me an eggnog, heavy on the nog. I was still dressed in my boating attire and sailor's hat and looked like something the cat dragged in.

But Linda seemed to be spell bound as I told them my account of what I had just experienced.

Jack was a great storyteller himself but he also knew when to relinquish the floor. So as I talked Jack kept the eggnogs rolling.

Now Linda was just 18 and one of those girls that looked young for her age and even when she turned fifty she was still going to look young. She had green eyes and a smile that was infectious and flirtations all at the same time.

She was wearing a short but tight green silk dress that hugged her body like a politician hugging a campaign contribution. She was a vivacious flirt and had no qualms about sitting very close to me as I spun my tale. She seemed to be the kind of girl who appreciated an older mature man, I was after all going to be 21 in just 18 months and she seemed to be more than interested and maybe was even intrigued with my captain's persona as I was still wearing my captain's hat and pea coat. As I continued my story she moved even closer and I could feel her nylon clad leg rubbing up next to mine as I gazed into her perfect twinkling green eyes.

After telling them my tale, I asked Linda what she thought about an artist that might be going through a "pasta" stage in his career. She thought that was fantastic and mentioned she was half Italian and said she was considering changing her major to art. And with that I thought for a second about that cold forlorn bay I had just returned from and how fast my mood had changed. In just a few hours I had gone from the coldest bleakest place on earth to, well, Linda. And after some more talk and some passionate handholding,

I somehow knew that I would not be spending New Years Eve alone. A new song popped into to me head, "Linda Bells, Linda Bells, Linda all the way."

The End   **Captain William Czappa**

Other books by this author are available on Amazon.com and eBay search for czappa

Trial, Tribulations and Triumphs of running a Small business.
Why I sold my business after 35 years full of stories about my employees and business tips.

Tech Techniques
A book about his 50 years in the repair industry. Rules that you learn the hard way.

Holidaze
A book of his humor short stories about vacations and Holidaze while growing up in Culver City Ca. and being a single parent.

Assembled in America

A book about is career as and artist with autobiography and 50 photos of his work with explanations.

eBay Users Handbook

After doing eBay for over 18 years, I thought I would share all the tips and techniques I had learned. And offer a step by step user guide to make the first time eBay seller a pro right from the start.

The Carpenter   *2007*

www.ingramcontent.com/pod-product-compliance
Lightning Source LLC
Chambersburg PA
CBHW071601220526
45469CB00003B/1088